ESTABLISHED

Building on...

Achievement in Year 9 English

Jenny Thomas and Diane White

NELSON
CENGAGE Learning

Australia • Brazil • Japan • Korea • Mexico • Singapore • Spain • United Kingdom • United States

Building On ... Achievement in Year 9 English ESTABLISHED
1st Edition
Jenny Thomas
Diane White

Book and cover design: Book Design Ltd
Typesetter: Book Design Ltd
Production controller: Siew Han Ong
Reprint: Natalie Orr

Any URLs contained in this publication were checked for currency during the production process. Note, however, that the publisher cannot vouch for the ongoing currency of URLs.

Acknowledgements
Our grateful thanks to all past and present colleagues who have so generously shared their expertise, creativity and resources. English departments thrive on your collegiality.

The authors and publisher wish to thank the following people and organisations for permission to use the resources in this textbook. Every effort has been made to contact all copyright owners of material used in this book. In most cases this was successful and copyright is acknowledged as requested. Owners of any work reproduced here for which permission has not been cleared, please contact the publisher.

Extracts and full text (pages 62–64) from 'All Summer in a Day' by Ray Bradbury, reprinted by permission of Don Congdon Associates, Inc, copyright 1954, renewed 1982 by Ray Bradbury; page 14 S. Enright; page 16 'The Boxer' by Emma Payne; page 17 extract from 'Sunday Morning' by Lauris Edmond; page 24 newspaper article 'Ancient rituals usher in New Year' by Errol Kiong reprinted with permission from North Shore Times Jan 31, 2003; page 26 Retailworld Resourcing for the advertisement; page 28 'Dinghy at the Water's Edge' by John Geraets; page 40 The Good, the Bad and the Dusty courtesy Jet Magazine New Zealand; page 44 'Footrot Flats' cartoon strip courtesy Murray Ball, Meryl Howell; page 45 extract from G-Force courtesy Tania Roxborogh; page 50 NZ Beef and Lamb for the advertisement; page 54 'Fone Filosofy' by Louise Phyn; page 60 North Shore City Council for the 'Understanding Our Environment' advertisement; page 66 Winter and Summer in Bannockburn by Oliver Miller; Live-wire Learning (www.livewirelearning.co.nz) for selected grammar examples.

For product information and technology assistance,
in Australia call **1300 790 853**;
in New Zealand call **0800 449 725**

For permission to use material from this text or product, please email
aust.permissions@cengage.com

National Library of New Zealand Cataloguing-in-Publication Data
Thomas, Jenny.
Building on-- achievement in year 9 English : established / Jenny Thomas and Diane White.
ISBN 978-0-17-019593-5
1. English language—Rhetoric—Juvenile literature. 2. English language—Composition and exercises—Juvenile literature. [1. English language—Rhetoric. 2. English language—Composition and exercises.] I. White, Diane. II. Title.
808.042—dc 22

Cengage Learning Australia
Level 7, 80 Dorcas Street
South Melbourne, Victoria Australia 3205

Cengage Learning New Zealand
Unit 4B Rosedale Office Park
331 Rosedale Road, Albany, North Shore 0632, NZ

For learning solutions, visit **cengage.com.au**

Printed in China by RR Donnelley Asia Printing Solutions Limited.
4 5 6 7 8 9 10 18 17 16 15 14

Contents

Language activities from *How to … Achieve in Year 9 English*   4

Blank storyboard from *How to … Achieve in Year 9 English*   12

Looking at speechwriting   14

Focus 1

Unit 1	Understanding poetry	16
Unit 2	Creative writing	18
Unit 3	Your school library	20
Unit 4	Theme essay	22
Unit 5	Written close reading	24
Unit 6	Visual close reading	26
Unit 7	Understanding poetry	28
Unit 8	Formal writing – wind energy: yes or no?	30
Unit 9	Creative writing	32
Unit 10	Written close reading	34
Unit 11	Creating character notes	36
Unit 12	Poetry writing – Diamantes	38
Unit 13	Analyse a review	40
Unit 14	Making a visual image	42
Unit 15	Visual close reading	44
Unit 16	Character essay	46
Unit 17	Speech planning	48
Unit 18	Visual close reading	50
Unit 19	Sentences make sense	52
Unit 20	Understanding poetry	54
Unit 21	Speech marks	56
Unit 22	Who makes movies?	58
Unit 23	Visual close reading	60
Unit 24	Putting it all together	62
Unit 25	Putting it all together	66
Refill pages for your own work		69–80

Focus 2

Imagery	17
Prefixes and suffixes	19
Library mix and match	21
Library quiz	21
Clichés	23
Apostrophes	25
Pronouns in advertising	27
Poetry recap	29
Colloquial language and slang	31
Spelling	33
Homonyms and homophones	35
Paragraphing	37
Adjectives	39
How to write … a film review	41
Visual and verbal techniques	43
Recap parts of speech	45
Verbs and adverbs	47
Speechwriting techniques	49
Punctuation practice	51
Prepositions and conjunctions	53
New languages – texting and emailing	55
Formal writing	55
Proofreading	57
Pronouns	59
Word origin	61

This section connects directly to the first chapter of the accompanying textbook *How to ... Achieve in Year 9 English*. You may like to use this to make your life easier.

Group 1: Parts of Speech

Check it

A noun is a naming word. There are four main types of nouns: common, proper, abstract and collective.

Identify the **common noun(s)** in the following sentences by either circling them in blue pen or using a highlighter.

1 The athlete won the race.
2 The cyclist climbed the hill.
3 The boy plays tennis.

Identify the **proper noun(s)** in the following sentences by either circling them in blue pen or using a highlighter.

4 My sister Jennifer is a lawyer.
5 Matthew is a very good cyclist and he rides for the province of Southland.
6 Mum and Dad went to Melbourne for the Commonwealth Games last month.

Identify the **abstract noun(s)** in the following sentences by either circling them in blue pen or using a highlighter.

7 The speaker showed her concern.
8 Tania's honesty was noticed by her friends.
9 Colin has a short temper.
10 Ed's tennis shows great skill and promise.

Identify the **collective noun(s)** in the following sentences by either circling them in blue pen or using a highlighter.

11 The rugby team practised every night before the big game.
12 I went to hear the orchestra play.
13 The boy looked carefully at the photo of a pack of wolves.
14 The principal addressed his staff for the last time.

Pronouns

The pronoun takes the place of a noun.

Identify the **personal pronoun(s)** in the following sentences by either circling them in blue pen or using a highlighter.

1 Kate and I went to the circus last night.
2 At the circus we saw the juggling monkeys.
3 The boys found that the big top was full when they arrived. The tent was much bigger than us.
4 Soon the clowns came out and made us laugh at the funny tricks they did.
5 Kate and I ate popcorn while we watched the movie. It filled us up.
6 You should have seen the clever little monkey ride the bike. Kate loved him.
7 The trapeze artists were brave. They were swinging high up in the roof of the tent. It looked very dangerous.
8 Jim was the ringmaster. He was kind but the animals still obeyed him.
9 One of the clowns sat beside me and grabbed my handbag. I yelled at him and told him the handbag was mine.
10 Kate said she would join the circus if they let her.

Adjectives

Adjectives describe nouns and pronouns.

Identify the **adjective(s)** in the following sentences by either circling them in blue pen or using a highlighter.

1 He did not know what could have caused this terrible state of affairs.
2 Golan scratched his thick, red beard.
3 He wondered where to start to solve this strange mystery.
4 Just then he heard a faint, thin cry.
5 He hurried towards the solid, brick house opposite him.
6 'Hello!' he rudely shouted, as he pushed open the creaky door.
7 From out of the dusty darkness the small voice answered nervously.
8 'Are you a kind friend or nasty foe?' he asked.
9 'This dessert is really delicious,' said Mum.
10 The child spat out the sour lemon.

ISBN 9780170195935

Comparatives and superlatives

A comparative compares two things. A superlative compares more than two things and describes the best.

Identify the **comparative(s)** and **superlative(s)** in the following sentences by either circling them in blue pen or using a highlighter.

1 The children were happier than they had ever thought possible.
2 She cried out in the smallest voice imaginable.
3 The more he practised, the more competent he became.
4 The strangest thing of all was the door was still locked.
5 The weather is becoming sunnier and warmer by the day.
6 As we dived deeper, the colours and variety of sealife grew.

Verbs

A verb is a 'doing' or an 'action' word.

Identify the **verb(s)** in the following sentences by either circling them in blue pen or using a highlighter.

1 Charlotte rode her bike to the shops.
2 She entered the dairy and asked for an ice cream.
3 The ice cream was hokey-pokey and it tasted wonderful.
4 Charlotte spotted her Aunt Elisabeth across the road.
5 She waved to her and called out, 'Hi, auntie!' in a loud voice.
6 Her Aunt looked across at her and waved back.
7 'I am on my way to your house,' she said as she came close to Charlotte.

Adverbs

Adverbs are words that tell us more about verbs. They answer the question 'How?', 'When?' or 'Where?'.

Identify the **adverb(s)** in the following sentences by either circling them in blue pen or using a highlighter.

1 The boy ran quickly around the corner.
2 The very sick child was taken to the hospital.
3 Rebecca behaved stupidly.
4 The dog hungrily ate his dinner.
5 We are coming now.
6 Don't eat so quickly.
7 She crept silently towards the door.
8 I have been waiting here for 30 minutes!
9 The rain was welcome after the long drought.
10 The hikers were lost because of the heavy rain.

Conjunctions

Conjunctions are connecting words that join two or more sentences into a single sentence. They can also join words, phrases or clauses.

Identify the **conjunction(s)** in the following sentences by either circling them in blue pen or using a highlighter.

1 She speaks French and German fluently.
2 I've been learning French for five years yet I am still far from fluent.
3 Take a thermos flask and a cake of chocolate with you.
4 You can have the Holden or the Honda; it is your choice.
5 'If you can't stand the heat, get out of the kitchen,' said the politician.

Prepositions

Prepositions are the 'small words' that usually relate two words or groups of words to one another.

Identify the **preposition(s)** in the following sentences by either circling them in blue pen or using a highlighter.

1 The TV news begins at 6.00.
2 You'll find the supplementary copy on the shelf.
3 The kids were running through the bush.
4 Brittany picked up the *Dolly* magazine.
5 Statistics New Zealand conducted a census in 2005.

Let's recap parts of speech

Read the extract from the Ray Bradbury short story *All Summer in a Day* below and complete the activities that follow:

But she remembered and stood quietly apart from all of them and watched the patterning windows. And once, a month ago, she had refused to shower in the school shower rooms, had clutched her hands to her ears and over her head, screaming the water mustn't touch her head. So after that, dimly, dimly, she sensed it, she was different and they knew her difference and kept away. There was talk that her father and mother were taking her back to Earth next year; it seemed vital to her that they do so, though it would mean the loss of thousands of dollars to her family. And so, the children hated her for all these reasons of big and little consequence. They hated her pale snow face, her waiting silence, her thinness, and her possible future.

ISBN 9780170195935

1 A **noun** is a naming word. There are four main types of nouns: common, proper, collective and abstract.
   - Highlight an example of five common nouns.
   - Highlight an example of a proper noun.
   - Highlight an example of an abstract noun.

2 The **pronoun** takes the place of a noun. List the pronouns used in this extract. _____

_____

3 **Adjectives** describe nouns and pronouns. They are often called describing words. List the adjectives used in this

   extract. _____

4 A **verb** is a 'doing' or an 'action' word. List the verbs used in this extract.

_____

_____

5 **Adverbs** are words that tell us more about verbs. They give us more information about how, when, or where
   something is done. Can you find an example of an adverb in the extract above?

_____

6 **Conjunctions** are connecting words that join two or more sentences into a single sentence. List the conjunctions
   used in this extract. _____

7 **Prepositions** are the 'small words' that usually relate two words or groups of words to one another. List the
   prepositions used in this extract. _____

Group 2: Punctuation

Punctuation marks make the written text easier to read and understand.
Without punctuation, writing would not make sense.

Capital letters

1 **Sentences always start with capital letters.**
2 **Proper nouns need a capital letter.**
3 **The main words in titles of books, films, plays, songs and so on are written using capital letters.**

Correct the following sentences using **capital letters** where appropriate.
1 we visited napier in the school holidays.
2 doctor barrett explained that it was necessary for me to have a blood test.
3 yesterday my mum took me to pak'nsave to buy the ingredients for my birthday dinner.
4 my younger brother, jack, is a pain in the neck!
5 sir peter blake is an inspiration to all new zealanders.
6 our prime minister will visit waitangi on the 6th of february.

Full stop

The full stop (.) shows the reader when one sentence (one idea) is complete.

Correct the following sentences using **capital letters** and **full stops** where appropriate.
1 i have decided to take drama, geography and graphics next year
2 megan was the best ballet dancer i knew she was incredibly light on her feet
3 i am in year 9 and go to whangarei girls' high school i am in the junior touch rugby team
4 my favourite book is 'to kill a mockingbird' by harper lee i had to read it in english last year
5 tomorrow is our last game of soccer for the season i am not going to miss getting up early on a saturday morning

Question mark

The question mark is a sign that a question has been asked.

Exclamation mark

The exclamation mark is a sign that shows strong emotion, or when somebody is shouting.

Correct the following sentences by placing a **full stop, exclamation** or **question mark** where appropriate.
1 I am the baby of the family
2 I am so scared
3 Why do we need an education
4 For goodness sake would you hurry up
5 Where are you going
6 What will happen next
7 It is important that you arrive on time
8 Do we have to go Mum it is soooo boring
9 We have been in the car a long time how much further to go
10 Ouch That really hurt

ISBN 9780170195935

The comma

The comma shows links in a sentence as well as separating items within a sentence.

Each sentence needs one or two **commas**. Put them in the correct place(s).

1 I left the house at six hoping to reach the sports ground before seven o'clock.
2 Sue went to the shop to buy candles balloons and streamers for the party.
3 My mother's favourite band Split Enz is on the TV tonight.
4 After playing rugby in the morning he went to play soccer in the afternoon.
5 Chess is a fascinating game more challenging than draughts.
6 My brother who is the hungriest person in the world just loves pizza.

Apostrophe

Apostrophes can be used to show contractions or possession.

Write out the **contraction** for the following phrases in the space provided.

1 would have _____
2 does not _____
3 they are _____
4 do not _____
5 they will _____
6 have not _____

Decide whether each sentence uses the **apostrophe** in the correct place or not.
If it does, write T (True); if not, write F (False).

1 He's the fastest runner in the school.
2 Im going to the movies' tonight.
3 Where's the cheese?
4 He is very sick and shouldnt be going to school today.
5 Cant I have some more pocket money, Mum?
6 The waka was put back in its resting place after the traditional welcome.
7 Weve been to the beach today.
8 The team owes its win to the goalkeeper's skill.

Inverted commas/speech marks

Inverted commas/speech marks are used at the beginning and end of groups of words that are actually *spoken*.

Decide whether each sentence uses **speech marks** in the correct place or not.
If it does, write T (True); if not, write F (False).

1 Miss Price said, 'There will be no homework over this weekend.'
2 'Could you pass the sugar please, Ben'?
3 Martin Luther King said, 'I have a dream!'
4 Rebecca leapt up. 'What do you think you are doing?' 'You should be at school!'
5 A voice came over the airport speaker system. Would Karen O'Reilly please make her way to the gate.

Let's recap word classes

Use a blue pen to punctuate the following extract from the Ray Bradbury short story *All Summer in a Day.* (We've left a bit of it there to help you out.)

now dont go too far called the teacher after them youve only two hours you know You wouldnt want to get caught out

But they were running and turning their faces up to the sky and feeling the sun on their cheeks like a warm iron they were taking off their jackets and letting the sun burn their arms

oh, its better than the sun lamps isn't it

much, much better

they stopped running and stood in the great jungle that covered Venus, that grew and never stopped growing, tumultuously, even as you watched it

ISBN 9780170195935

Check it

A sentence is a group of words that together express a complete thought.

Select to which **sentence type** these sentences belong. Choose from either *simple*, *compound* or *complex*.

1 Golf is a great game. _____

2 Get some milk and top up the petrol, please. _____

3 She cut my hair but I didn't like it. _____

4 Ancient Egyptians had good dentists. _____

5 This coffee is strong because I ordered an espresso. _____

Select to which **sentence type** this sentence belongs. Choose from either *imperative sentence*, *exclamatory sentence*, *minor sentence* or *rhetorical question*.

1 Leave me alone, please. _____

2 It's a goal! _____

3 Very tasty, thanks. _____

4 Do you think I'm an idiot? _____

5 Is she for real? _____

6 Take the next road on the right. _____

7 Fantastic! _____

Let's recap syntax

In this extract from the short story *All Summer in a Day* three sentences have been highlighted in bold. They are a minor sentence, a compound sentence and a simple sentence. Which is which?

'Ready?'
'Ready.'
'Now?
'Soon.' _____
'Do the scientists really know? Will it happen today, will it?'
'Look, look; see for yourself !'
The children pressed to each other like so many roses, so many weeds, intermixed, peering out for a look at the hidden sun.
It rained. _____
It had been raining for seven years; thousands upon thousands of days compounded and filled from one end to the other with rain, with the drum and gush of water, with the sweet crystal fall of showers and the concussion of storms so heavy they were tidal waves come over the islands. **A thousand forests had been crushed under the rain and grown up a thousand times to be crushed again.** And this was the way life was forever on the planet Venus, and this was the schoolroom of the children of the rocket men and women who had come to a raining world to set up civilization and live out their lives.
'It's stopping, it's stopping!' _____
'Yes, yes!'

The simile

A simile is a direct comparison that always contains the words 'as' or 'like'.

Decide whether the following sentences include a **simile** or not by writing T (True) or F (False) in each box.

1 The baby was like a pig when it ate.

2 The house was as solid as a rock.

3 He's a solid kind of person.

ISBN 9780170195935

4 The house is built on solid rock.

5 She danced as delicately as a butterfly.

6 That's a piggy way of eating.

7 Excitement swelled up inside them.

8 The burglar moved with cat-like stealth through the garden.

The metaphor

A metaphor is a comparison which does not use 'like' or 'as'.

Decide whether the following sentences include a **metaphor** or not by writing T (True) or F (False) in each box.

1 He is like a pig when he eats.

2 He is a pig when he eats.

3 The soldiers were herded into the cave.

4 The young girl sang like a nightingale.

5 'You're a wise owl,' said the teacher to his student.

6 The farmer ploughed his paddock.

7 The ship ploughed through the waves.

Identify the metaphor in the following sentences by either underlining or highlighting the phrase.

8 The bedclothes were hills on her unmade bed.

9 The thief was a silent shadow lurking in the darkest corners.

10 A silver ball hung in the night sky.

11 Her anger was a searing, hot blast through the whole room.

12 The heavy rain was a drum.

Personification

Personification is where a non-living object is given living qualities, writing of it as if it were a living person.

Decide whether the following sentences include a **personification** or not by writing T (True) or F (False) in each box.

1 The wind was attacking the flowers.

2 The trees sighed happily in the breeze.

3 As the sun set like a huge apricot, George walked the trail.

4 The waves were large animals looming above him.

5 Bored blowflies whine monotonously in the still air.

6 The colourful flowers shimmered like exquisite lace in the summer breeze.

7 The butterflies flitted joyfully around the beautiful garden.

8 The moss was a green cloak enveloping the big rock.

9 The creeping shadows lurked in the dark corners.

10 The clouds were soft and wispy like feathers.

Alliteration

Alliteration is the repetition of consonant sounds at the beginning of words placed closely together to create a sound echo.

Decide whether the following phrases use **alliteration** or not by writing T (True) or F (False) in each box.

1 Friend or foe!

2 law and order

3 criminal conspiracy

4 Fish – the family dish.

5 pickled peppers

6 sound spectacular

7 Windy Wellington

Getting tricky!

8 friendly photographer

9 the circling cat

10 the capable citizen

11 The knight felt nauseous.

ISBN 9780170195935

Identify the **alliteration** in the following sentences by either underlining or highlighting the repeated consonant sound.

1   He ran to the rocks.
2   The rabbits rushed raucously around their hutch.
3   The cat silently stalked its unsuspecting prey.
4   The snow drifted like leaves onto the lawn.
5   The stream rambled and burbled breathlessly through the field.
6   The snake slipped and slithered menacingly through the field.
7   The photographer flashed and filmed effusively.
8   The butcher's face became red and ruddy, carrying the heavy rump and rissoles.

Assonance

Assonance is the repetition of vowel sounds. The trick is not to think of it as the same *letter*, but the same *sound*.

Decide whether the following sentences include **assonance** or not by writing T (True) or F (False) in each box.

1   He heard a dull, pulsating sound.

2   A large crack ripped through the night and woke Nathan.

3   She gazed at a sea of green.

4   'What was that?' he said, as he sat bolt upright in bed.

5   His thin limbs were delicate.

6   The only sound now was the buzzing of a large blowfly butting up against the window,
    behind which a street lamp glowed.

7   They walked down the wind-dried road.

8   The wind sighed through the trees.

9   I stood upon the shore.

10 Troubles rested on my shoulders.

Onomatopoeia

Onomatopoeia uses words that imitate and reproduce real-life sounds and actions.

Decide whether the following sentences include **onomatopoeia** or not by writing T (True) or F (False) in each box.

1   We could hear the stormy sea booming through the caves.

2   The supermarket trolley went careering noisily down the aisle.

3   We heard huge clangs when the church bell was rung.

4   The boy leapt into the pool with a huge displacement of water.

5   We could hear the crunch of their footsteps when they walked along the stony path.

6   The waves landed heavily on the beach at the height of the storm.

Rhyme

Rhyme is the repetition of final vowel and consonant sounds in words. Two types of rhyme you may see at this level are full and internal.

Decide whether the following sentences include **rhyme** or not by writing T (True) or F (False) in each box.

1   The wind-dried road stretched far into the distance.

2   You do the crime, you do the time.

3   A dull, pulsating sound was heard.

4   The rain in Spain falls mainly on the plain.

5   His thin limbs were delicate.

6   Do not conceal thy radiant eye
    The starlight of serenest skies

7   The fair breeze blew, the white foam flew,
    The furrow followed free

10

ISBN 9780170195935

8   I watch him striding lank behind
     His clashing team.

9   Wee Willie Winkie ran through the town
     Upstairs and downstairs in his nightgown.

10   It cracked and growled, and roared and howled.

Rhythm

Rhythm is a particular pattern that suggests movement or pace.

1   Learn the following verse from Jack Prelutsky's poem *The Witch*. Listen to the rhythm. Note especially how the last line has to be said slowly and this is to emphasise the witch's wickedness.

> She comes by night, in fearsome flight,
> in garments black as pitch,
> the queen of doom upon her broom,
> the wild and wicked witch.

2   Learn the following verse from *The Highwayman*. Listen to the rhythm. Note especially the regular sound of the galloping horse.

> The wind was a torrent of darkness among the gusty trees,
> The moon was a ghostly galleon tossed upon cloudy seas,
> The road was a ribbon of moonlight, over the purple moor,
> And the highwayman came riding –
> Riding – riding –
> The highwayman came riding, up to the old inn-door.

Let's recap figures of speech

Read the extract from the Ray Bradbury short story *All Summer in a Day* below. Then write one example of each of the identified poetic terms.

Margot stood apart from them, from these children who could never remember a time when there wasn't rain and rain and rain. They were all nine years old, and if there had been a day, seven years ago, when the sun came out for an hour and showed its face to the stunned world, they could not recall. Sometimes, at night, she heard them stir, in remembrance, and she knew they were dreaming and remembering gold or a yellow crayon or a coin large enough to buy the world with. She knew they thought they remembered a warmness, like a blushing in the face, in the body, in the arms and legs and trembling hands. But then they always awoke to the tatting drum, the endless shaking down of clear bead necklaces upon the roof, the walk, the gardens, the forests, and their dreams were gone.

All day yesterday they had read in class about the sun. About how like a lemon it was, and how hot. And they had written small stories or essays or poems about it:

I think the sun is a flower,
That blooms for just one hour.

That was Margot's poem, read in a quiet voice in the still classroom while the rain was falling outside.

'Aw, you didn't write that!' protested one of the boys.

'I did,' said Margot. 'I did.'

'William!' said the teacher.

But that was yesterday. Now the rain was slackening, and the children were crushed in the great thick windows.

'Where's teacher?'

'She'll be back.'

'She'd better hurry, we'll miss it!'

They turned on themselves, like a feverish wheel, all tumbling spokes. Margot stood alone.

1   Simile   _____

2   Metaphor   _____

3   Personification   _____

4   Alliteration   _____

5   Onomatopoeia   _____

ISBN 9780170195935

17

Storyboard

Use the storyboard below to complete the activity on pages 128–130 of *How to ... Achieve in Year 9 English*.

Shot No.		Shot Type:
		Dialogue/Soundtrack:

Shot No.		Shot Type:
		Dialogue/Soundtrack:

Shot No.		Shot Type:
		Dialogue/Soundtrack:

Shot No.		Shot Type:
		Dialogue/Soundtrack:

Shot No.		Shot Type:
		Dialogue/Soundtrack:

Shot No.		Shot Type:
		Dialogue/Soundtrack:

ISBN 9780170195935

Shot No.		Shot Type:
		Dialogue/Soundtrack:

Shot No.		Shot Type:
		Dialogue/Soundtrack:

Shot No.		Shot Type:
		Dialogue/Soundtrack:

Shot No.		Shot Type:
		Dialogue/Soundtrack:

Shot No.		Shot Type:
		Dialogue/Soundtrack:

Shot No.		Shot Type:
		Dialogue/Soundtrack:

13

ISBN 9780170195935

Looking at speechwriting

This activity connects to page 140 of *How to ... Achieve in Year 9 English*.

It is useful to look at the structure of someone else's work before you begin writing your own speech. Annotate the speech where it demonstrates use of:

- personal pronouns
- statistics
- metaphor
- rhetorical questions
- bridging words and phrases
- ironic humour
- links to its audience
- links between introduction and conclusion
- where voice intonation, gesture and eye contact might be particularly effective.

Let me tell you about something I've been doing for almost 13 years now, something which has, in fact, been a significant focus of virtually my entire life up to this point. It's an endeavour that is almost finished; a long journey that has all but reached its destination. What is it that I've been doing for so long and with such commitment and dedication?

Preparing to become a TEENAGER!

As I've already mentioned, I've put a lot of time and effort into this project. In recent months I've been doing some serious research into the facts, figures and statistics of teenage-hood, putting the finishing touches to my 13 year preparation to enter this new phase in my life. After all, I want to be as well prepared as I can be for turning 13.

I've discovered that the word "teenager" only began to be used after World War Two. I consider myself very fortunate to live in an age when I can actually be a teenager! Just imagine ... If I'd lived 70 years ago, I'd be about to become a "youth"! Doesn't sound nearly as much fun, does it?

What other important, eye-opening information have I discovered in my research?

Well, I've found that New Zealand teenagers are more likely than other groups to live in urban areas rather than rural communities. And that the main cause of teenage death in our country is road accidents. That's sad, but sadder still is the fact that the second main cause of death is suicide.

Another thing I've found is that 8% of New Zealand teenagers have a disability which limits their daily activity, and that 6% of teenagers do some vigorous physical activity at least once a week.

ISBN 9780170195935

These sorts of facts are interesting, and help me get an overview of teenage life in New Zealand, but facts and information alone will not make me a success at being a teenager. There are numerous important skills I need to learn, and areas in which I need to develop, and it's these things I've been working on so hard for so long. I have been extremely fortunate to grow up with an older brother and sister who have provided me with expert, full-time, on-the-job training in the intricacies of teenage living; they've put me through rigorous courses in such important matters as teenage bedroom care.

I'm embarrassed to admit it, but by nature I'm a very tidy person ... and of course that would just never do for a fully-fledged teenager. I used to always keep my bedroom in an immaculate condition and if such behaviour were to continue into my teenage years, naturally it would result in my immediate expulsion from the teenagers' union! I have had an expert in my brother to help me overcome this problem, and I've really been working hard at becoming sufficiently messy to qualify for teenage-hood. Certainly my mother has noticed the difference, which is very gratifying! My brother has been a wonderful role model for me in this area, and although I can't yet get close to the level of untidiness that he maintains in his bedroom, seemingly without any effort at all, I really am improving my ability at keeping my room in a shambles 24/7! I'm hoping eventually to be able to pass on my skills to my two younger sisters, and be the sort of example for them that my brother has been for me. After all, isn't that what families are for?

Another crucial area I've been working on is my intellectual development. As everyone knows, the major task of any self-respecting teenager is to educate their parents. Parents of teenagers seem to have a special knack of saying and doing foolish things, which completely embarrass their children! Part of a teenager's job description is to know everything, so you can try and educate your parents and make them at least passably sensible! So I've been working very hard to build up my knowledge pool, and am pleased to say that I now know just about everything, and am almost ready to begin my parents' re-training.

The countdown has now begun. Only four days to go until I become a teenager. And I think I'm just about all set! It's been a long period of preparation, but I've covered all the bases and I'm feeling pretty confident that I'll be a natural!!

ISBN 9780170195935

Week _____ Date for completion _____

Parent's sig. _____ Teacher's sig. _____

Focus 1: Understanding poetry

The Boxer

Simile _____

Metaphor

The great iron figure crouches,
Scabs like flowers on his knees,
And his chest is like a mountain
And his legs are thick as trees.

Simile _____

He spits blood like a cherub
In a fountain spouting foam,
Ringed around by swimming ropes
And punters going home.

Simile _____

Broken-knuckled, shiny-eyed.
Battered, bruised, and wet
With droplets like cold rubies,
And laced with bitter sweat.

Alliteration

Alliteration

He crouches in a corner
In his pool of sparkling red
And dreads the jeers which soon will fall
Like blows upon his head.

Simile _____

By Emma Payne

Similes

Annotate the highlighted simile that best describes each of the following features of the boxer.

A   He has a previous knee injury.
B   He has lost the fight.
C   He has been injured in the fight.
D   He has worked out and trained.

Metaphor

Draw a line linking the metaphor box to the metaphor in the poem.

Alliteration

Draw a line linking each alliteration box to a different example.

Rhyme

Use a red pen to underline the pairs of rhyming words in each verse.

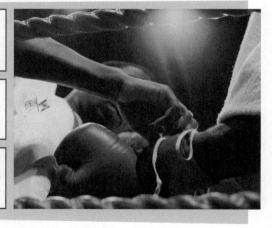

Vocabulary choice

You will no doubt have been told that poets are very careful with the words they choose to use. There are only 85 words in this poem and none of them arrived on the page by accident. Rather, the poet chose them for their effect, connotations, sound and so on. Choose three effective phrases from the poem and explain why each suits the poem.

1 _____

_____

2 _____

_____

3 _____

_____

ISBN 9780170195935

Focus 2: Imagery

You will hear your teacher talking about 'imagery'. Imagery in writing is descriptive language that usually appeals to the senses. The images may be formed by literal description or by figures of speech such as similes and metaphors.

When you look in a mirror, you see an image – a likeness of yourself. When you use a camera and take a picture of your friend, the photograph is an image of that person. If you write a description of your friend, you are creating an image of that person in words. In writing, an image is a picture made up from words.

Literal imagery refers to the pictures (or sense experiences), which mean exactly what they say. For example, 'The pale moon gleamed in a dark sky'. Everyone has seen the moon in the sky and so can picture this pretty easily.

Figurative imagery involves figures of speech. These 'figures' of speech may use comparisons or exaggeration. You need to use your imagination to understand the qualities that are being conveyed. Often one thing is described as being like something else, to help us imagine what the writer sees, feels, hears, thinks.

One of the most commonly used figures of speech is the simile. Similes are comparisons that use the words 'like' or 'as' to point out the comparison. For example, 'The pale moon gleamed in a dark sky, round as a white plate on a dark tablecloth.' Here you are asked to imagine the cold, white china of the plate and the dark, dense fabric of the cloth and then think more clearly of this particular moon in this particular sky.

Metaphors are also comparisons, which suggest one part of the comparison has some of the qualities of the other part. For example, 'My dad has sandpaper hands.' You know Dad's hands aren't really made of sandpaper but you can easily imagine his rough skin, can't you?

Personification is a special kind of metaphor that gives the qualities of a person or animal to something that is not a person. For example, 'The fog comes on little cat feet.' In this image the poet wants you to think of fog moving as *silently* as a cat. It is the lack of sound (not the furry feet) that is the shared quality.

Here is the first verse of a poem called *Sunday Morning* by New Zealand poet Lauris Edmond, which uses imagery to help you imagine a scene:

> Down at the corner dairy
> The Sunday morning sun
> Is yellow as a pancake
> Frying on the sky;
> Last night's litter
> Shuffles about in a gutter
> And the seedy little shop
> Stands up and wipes its chin
> Ready for the day's
> Business to begin.

You can identify the simile in the poem, 'sun/Is yellow as a pancake …' and the personification of the litter 'shuffling' and the shop 'stands up and wipes its chin'. Now use your imagination and ask yourself, what do the two things being compared in the simile have in common? The sun is yellow, so is the pancake. They're both hot. And maybe the pancake reminds the writer of morning, of breakfast time?

Personification can be a bit more difficult to 'get'. The writer says the litter shuffles about in a gutter. Why? Perhaps because it's aimless, has no value, is discarded; it belongs to yesterday, before this new start. Maybe it's to suggest there's a bit of a breeze this particular morning? Think things out as far as you can to fully appreciate why the writer has chosen particular words and phrases.

You do:

1 Try explaining this phrase about the shop yourself.   **And the seedy little shop / Stands up and wipes its chin**

_____

_____

_____

2 Imagery is used in both poetry and in prose writing. You choose your own way: write either a poem or a passage of descriptive writing.

Take a weather situation: imagine the weather is a person (old, young, angry, sad, serious, joker, male, female etc) and write about what it is trying to do to people, or the land, or the earth. Use your own experience of a weather situation to help you imagine what you want your reader to 'see'. Remember how simile, and metaphor and personification can help to create the image.

Here are some suggestions:

winter sunshine · gale · fog · sunshine · tornado · summer rainstorm · drought · tropical downpour · wind · blizzard

ISBN 9780170195935

17

Week _____ Date for completion _____

Parent's sig. _____ Teacher's sig. _____

Focus 1: Creative writing

So how do you tackle creative writing?

The process of writing does not change whether you have one hour or one week!

Just remember: Brainstorm → Draft → Write → Edit → Final copy

To help you get started and to ensure the following activity does not take you all week, we have suggested a time breakdown.

5 minutes	Look over the starters given. It is likely one or two will grab your attention. Look closely at this again and decide which gives you the most scope to work with.
10 minutes	Plan the story by brainstorming all your ideas. • Are you going to write a descriptive or narrative piece? • Think about the structure of the story to ensure you have a beginning, middle and end. • Think about your characters: are you using dialogue? • Think about some vocabulary and language techniques that will help improve your writing.
45 minutes	Write your piece, remembering to stick to the plan. A well-planned piece of writing will take you much less time to write than an unplanned piece.

Now leave your piece of writing. Come back to it at a later time and then ...

5 minutes	Reread your piece of writing.
15 minutes	Edit your piece. Check your: • Spelling • Vocabulary • Sentence structure: Can you make it more interesting? Vary it? • Opening • Closing.
15 minutes	Write the final copy of your story in the back of this book. Don't forget to check over your work once you have finished or get someone else to read it through. It is easy to miss little mistakes!

Starters

Choose one of the following starters to begin your work. Aim to write at least 250 words.

1 Rain penetrated the bush canopy ...
2 People swarmed onto the intersection as the crossing buzzer shrilled ...
3 The crowd watched with anticipation ...
4 Then it was Monday. In the space of a weekend the world had changed ...
5 Seventeen steps ...
6 I often felt left out ...
7 It was just my luck ...
8 It was really embarrassing ...
9 A pet with personality.
10 He walked to the front of the stage, slipped the rubber-band from around the book and slowly began to read.

Here are some clues to help you understand what your teacher is looking for.

- An original story that has a credible atmosphere, setting and storyline.
- A well-structured piece of writing that shows planning and thought.
- Effective expression and a variety of vocabulary.
- A piece of writing that shows you knew the end of the story before you began.
- A fluent writing style.
- Clear paragraphing.
- Correct expression and formal tone where appropriate.
- Only a few errors in grammar, punctuation and spelling.

Here are some clues to help you understand what the markers do not want to see.

- A piece of writing that is not very interesting.
- A piece of writing that is all one paragraph.
- A piece of writing that is too short.
- A lot of errors in grammar, punctuation and spelling.

ISBN 9780170195935

Focus 2: Prefixes and suffixes

The core of the word is called the root. What comes before is called the prefix. What comes after is called the suffix. We can change the meaning of a word by putting something before (prefix) or after (suffix) the root word.

Prefix	Root	Suffix
mis	use	
	use	less/ful
en	joy	ment

Prefixes

A prefix is a group of letters that is added to the front of a root word and changes its meaning.

Prefixes may create new words: **im**migrate   **pre**occupied

Prefixes may create antonyms: **un**friendly   **dis**satisfied

Don't worry if there is a 'double up' of letters when you join a prefix and root word together. In most cases neither the prefix nor the root word changes when you join them together.

For example: u**n** + **n**ecessary = u**nn**ecessary

Below is a chart of commonly used prefixes that modify (or change) the words they precede. Carefully read through the information and fill in the gaps with the correct information. The last lines have been left blank for you to find two of your own.

Prefix	Meaning	Usage		
aero	air	aeroplane	aerodynamic	
anti	against	anticlockwise		antisocial
fore		foreground	foresee	
mono		monotonous		
post	after	postwar		
		tricycle	triangle	
ultra	extreme			ultra-sensitive

Suffixes

A suffix is a group of letters that is added to the end of a root word and changes its meaning.

Here are a few examples of suffixes; all of them begin with a vowel:

able   al   ed   en   er   est   et   ing   ish   ist   ous   ive

When a word has one vowel before a single final consonant, double that consonant before adding the suffix.

For example: shop   shopp**ed**   shopp**ing**   shopp**er**
                 clap   clapp**ed**   clapp**ing**   clapp**er**

When the word ends in a silent e (which makes the vowel inside the word long), then drop that e before adding the ending.

For example: skate   skat**ed**   skat**ing**   skat**er**
                 arrive   arriv**ed**   arriv**ing**   arriv**al**

In the following sentences add a suffix to the underlined word to fill the space in the sentence.

1   You can <u>swim</u> in our pool if you are a strong _____.
2   Joy is <u>thin</u> but Judy is _____.
3   I <u>like</u> John; he's a _____ person.
4   <u>Write</u> clearly if you want to be a good _____.
5   This plum is <u>ripe</u> but that plum is _____.
6   <u>Big</u> trucks have the _____ wheels.
7   Go to the <u>shop</u> and collect my _____, please.
8   There is <u>danger</u> here. This place is _____.
9   A lot of <u>slime</u> in a pond means _____ weeds are there too.
10 Use a <u>screw</u> for _____ the top onto the table.

ISBN 9780170195935

Week _____ Date for completion _____

Parent's sig. _____ Teacher's sig. _____

Focus 1: Your school library

Draw the layout of your school library in the space below. Mark the following on your diagram:

Fiction	Non-fiction	Reference	Computers	Vertical File
Photocopier	Study desks	Casual seating	The librarian's office	Issues counter

Magazine and newspaper racks

ISBN 9780170195935

Focus 2a: Library mix and match

a		Reference book
b		Index
c		Encyclopedia
d		Catalogue
e		Fiction
f		Non-fiction
g		Dewey Decimal System
h		Due date
i		Author
j		Non-print
k		Keyword
l		Table of contents
m		Yearbook
n		Genre
o		Internet
p		Desk copy
q		Anthology

1. Novels, short stories, reading for pleasure.
2. A word indicating a main term or concept or subject discussed in a document; used in searching catalogues.
3. Books about facts – everything from A to Z.
4. Records, with detailed descriptions and location information, of the materials in a library collection. In most libraries it is stored on a computer.
5. An alphabetical detailed list of the names, places and subjects discussed in a book and the numbers of the pages on which each subject is treated. Usually found at the back of the book.
6. A list of the chapter or article titles in a book or journal. This is usually found at the beginning of a book after the title page.
7. A book such as a dictionary, encyclopedia or directory, which contains specific facts, data or other brief bits of information. It may not be borrowed.
8. An annual documentary, historical or memorial publication containing information about the previous year.
9. A library search term used to find examples of a type of literature, for example fantasy, mystery.
10. A reference book containing information on all subjects, or limited to a special field or subject. Sometimes in more than one volume.
11. A global network connecting millions of computers. This includes but is not limited to the World Wide Web. It can be used for e-mail and other functions.
12. The date by which borrowed materials must be returned to the library or renewed.
13. Books that are held by the librarians due to them being in high demand by students. Access is only allowed on a period-by-period basis.
14. A writer of a book, essay, story, play, poem or other work.
15. Materials published in a format other than print on paper, for example audio/video cassettes, CD-ROMs, DVDs.
16. A collection of poems, short stories or essays, by more than one author.
17. A system of classifying books and other materials by subject using a numerical system so that like materials are shelved next to each other.

Focus 2b : Library quiz

Use the resources in the library to find the answers to the following questions. You must use EACH of the following sources AT LEAST ONCE to find your answers.
- a reference book
- a non-fiction book
- an encyclopedia
- the Internet

Use the shaded column alongside the question to write which source you used to answer the question.
RB = reference book, ENC = encyclopedia, NF = non-fiction, INT = Internet.

1	When and where were the first Olympic Games held?
2	Why were they named the 'Olympic' Games?
3	How many rings are there on the Olympic flag?
4	Why were the colours of the rings of the Olympic flag chosen?
5	In which track and field event do athletes jump over obstacles?
6	How many Olympic Games have been held?
7	Explain the story behind the Olympic torch relay.
8	How many countries are eligible to compete in the Olympic Games?
9	Where were the last Olympic Games held?

10	Where will the next Olympic Games be held?
11	Name (and give the details of their sport and winnings) one famous Olympic medallist from each of the following era. 60s: 80s: 90s:
12	What were the original sports competed in at the first Olympic Games?
13	What is the newest sport to become part of the Olympic Games?
14	When did drug testing come into the Olympic Games?
15	Find one interesting piece of information about the Olympic Games that you have not already used to answer a question

ISBN 9780170195935

Week _____ Date for completion _____

Parent's sig. _____ Teacher's sig. _____

HINT FOR SUCCESS
It is important to use relevant quotations in your literary essays. You need to prove that you have a wide knowledge of the text.

Focus 1: Theme essay

This activity asks you to write a clear, detailed, thoughtful essay. Complete the information in the box below before you begin.

Title of text: _____ Author of text: _____

Let's recap how to write a literary essay

By now you will be aware of the basic structure you can use to write your essay.

Don't forget to use quotations to support your ideas. Go to page 98 of your *How to ...* textbook to remind yourself on how to best incorporate quotations in your essay.

Introduction

This paragraph should always:

- give the title and author (director, poet) of the text
- give the genre (novel, short story, poem, film)
- refer to the question.

Body paragraphs

The body of the essay is divided into paragraphs. How many will depend on the type of question you're asked. Generally a body paragraph should have:

- a topic sentence that clearly states what the paragraph will be about
- detail from the text
- relevant quotations
- explanation
- a sentence to link back to the original idea.

Conclusion

This will include:

- no new information (it shows a lack of prior planning)
- a restatement of the main point of your essay, strongly referring back to the question.

Let's have a look at the essay topic you have been given.

Describe an idea that interested you in the text. Explain why it interested you.

Using a red or blue pen, annotate the question with the following.

- Put brackets around each part of the question.
- Underline the key words in the question.

In this box decide upon the following things.

- List the possible themes you could use for this topic.
- For each theme brainstorm at least two reasons why it was interesting.
- Think about some of the following things: Is it relevant to you? Could you apply it to something you are going through? Is it topical to other people your age?

Theme	Reasons
1	1
	2
2	1
	2
3	1
	2

ISBN 9780170195935

Evaluate the information you have in your box (page 22). Hopefully one idea/theme stands out as being easier to write about than the others.

- Look through your idea/theme handouts/notes.
- Go back to the key places in the text and reread them. Take notes and copy suitable quotes.
- Use a different-colour pen to group and structure your information.

You should now be ready to begin writing your essay. Use your own refill to draft your work. Write the final copy of your essay in the back of this book.

Focus 2: Clichés

Clichés are expressions that have been used so often that they have lost their original effect. Phrases that have now become clichés often began as interesting and distinctive expressions, but, after being used over and over again, all their sparkle and originality have disappeared.

Clichés can be put into six types:

1 **Over-used adjectives**, such as:
   the *acid* test
   tumultuous applause

2 **Stale figures of speech**, such as:
   Her face was as red as a tomato
   He's as fat as a pig

3 **Over-worked quotations**, such as:
   'The lady doth protest too much' –
   Romeo and Juliet
   'Hasta la vista, baby' – *The Terminator*

4 **Worn-out foreign phrases**, such as:
   femme fatale
   terra firma
   persona non grata

5 **Too-familiar idiomatic and proverbial expressions**, such as:
   the writing on the wall
   make a clean sweep
   get down to the nitty-gritty
   at the end of the day

6 **Repetitious fashionable phrases**,
   such as:
   the generation gap
   Generation X
   the body beautiful

As students you are usually advised not to use the first stock phrase that comes to mind. Instead try to think of a fresh and personal way of using words. Your writing will be more original in style if you think of your own forms of expression.

> You might find your parents useful when doing the tasks in this Focus!

Take a look at the following expressions that have become clichés over the years. They may be used either literally (in the actual sense) or figuratively (to create an image for the reader).

For instance look at the expression 'The fledglings have left the nest.' The literal meaning for this is that the small birds have left their nest, that is, they have grown up and flown away. The figurative meaning of this expression is that the children have left the nest to make lives of their own, that is, grown up and left home.

Give the meaning of each of the following expressions.

A bolt from the blue _____

A fish out of water _____

To move the goal posts _____

To beat around the bush _____

Under a cloud _____

Under the weather _____

Under cover _____

Under canvas _____

English is full of these sorts of expressions. See how many you can think of or look up some that have the word 'cat' in them. There are at least 15!

_____

ISBN 9780170195935

Week _____ Date for completion _____

Parent's sig. _____ Teacher's sig. _____

Focus 1: Written close reading

By now you will have done some work honing your close reading skills. We assume you have worked through the exercises in the *How to ...* textbook. Let's recap how it suggests you approach close reading a written text.

Helpful hints

Before attempting a passage there are a few things we recommend you do before you attempt a passage:

1. Read the text carefully.

2. Scan the text for difficult or unfamiliar words or phrases. Work out the meanings for this vocabulary by using the context of the passage, consulting a dictionary or discussing the words with your teacher or classmates.

3. Read the text again. While reading the passage the following strategies may help you while you read the passage.
   - Ask questions about the text and answer them while reading.
   - Visualise what is happening in the text.

4. Work through the questions one at a time.

Ancient rituals usher in New Year

For the substantial Chinese community on the Shore, the Spring Festival, more commonly known as Chinese New Year, is the most important festival in the Chinese lunar calendar. ERROL KIONG reports on some practices associated with the lunar new year, and how the Shore's Chinese community are ushering in the Year of the Black Sheep tomorrow.

The Chinese sleep early on the fourth day of Chinese New Year so the mice can get married.

The mice have free run of the house for one night of the year, procreating, feasting and generally causing havoc, in the hope that they won't finish the house owner's rice stocks, says Chinese affairs commentator Terry Teng.

This is just one of the many observances of Chinese New Year, which falls on February 1.

It is the most important event in the Chinese lunar calendar and, like its Western equivalent, has many traditions and rituals.

Its origin is centuries old, too old to be traced. Also known as the Spring Festival, Chinese New Year ushers in the start of spring in China, with celebrations lasting 15 days.

Preparations tend to begin a month before when people start buying presents, decoration materials, food and clothing.

A frenzy of cleaning also ensues days before the New Year, when Chinese houses are cleaned from top to bottom to sweep away the bad luck of the previous year.

Doors and windows are given a new coat

GOOD TIDINGS: *A Chinese spring scroll bearing congratulations for the new year.*

of paint, usually in red, an auspicious colour signifying wealth and luck.

Red scrolls bearing traditional themes of happiness, prosperity and peace for the coming year are then placed on doors and windows on New Year's Eve.

He still observes many of the more obscure rituals of the spring festival. The columnist for Auckland's Chinese-language newspapers and author of six books about New Zealand, feels it's important to keep traditions alive.

One New Year tradition is to not sweep or clean the house during the first five days, as it signifies sweeping luck out the door. Mr Teng says rubbish must be swept behind the door and kept there until after the fifth day.

In fact, no cooking and cleaning is to be done, only eating, drinking and having fun, says Mr Teng.

The Chinese-born and Taiwan-educated law professor says the first day is of special importance to the young as it is the day they visit their elders to receive 'hung bao' or red packets containing money.

Children and unmarried adults receive the red packets, and the whole family travel from door to door visiting relatives and

neighbours. At Chinese New Year, grudges are cast aside and relationships start afresh.

Chinese tradition has always seen married couples live with the groom's parents. Mr Teng says the second day is for married daughters to spend the day with their parents.

People rest early on the fourth day (for the mice), allowing them to save up their energy for celebrations of the fifth day, which kick off with a bang, literally.

Fireworks and firecrackers are let off, usually to the accompaniment of dragon and lion dances.

Of the many observances associated with the lunar new year, none is more important than New Year's Eve dinner.

Every family member gathers from far and near for the occasion. For the many migrant families here, it is easier said than done, Mr Teng says.

In New Zealand, Chinese families are extending their homes and New Year's Eve feast to friends and students without families here. Mr Teng, his wife Tina and daughter Ping Ping will have up to 25 people over for New Year's Eve dinner.

He might even have a barbecue, weather permitting, to cater for the huge number of people.

But some things simply must not be left off the dinner table on New Year's Eve. Seafood will feature in abundance. Delicacies include prawns, signifying liveliness and happiness, dried oysters, for good tidings, and raw fish salad for good luck and prosperity.

The 15th day is marked with the Festival of Lanterns, with a celebration of singing, dancing and lantern shows.

On the surface

1. What is the Chinese New Year also known as? _____

2. Why are Chinese homes cleaned thoroughly before New Year? _____

3. Which colour is given special significance during the New Year season? _____

4a How long do the celebrations for Chinese New Year last? _____

ISBN 9780170195935

4b What special traditions are observed on which days? _____

_____

_____

_____

5 Why does Mr Teng open his house to so many for his New Year's Eve dinner?_____

6 Even the food served on New Year's Eve has special significance. Give three examples.

_____

Technical

7 Find the cliché in the paragraph beginning 'People rest early …'. How is it connected to the next paragraph?

_____

8 Explain clearly why Mr Teng has been interviewed as part of this article. _____

_____

9 Why do you think the journalist began his article explaining a tradition involving mice?

_____

_____

Search and think

10 Which two paragraphs does the photo best match? Why? _____

_____

11 Why would a community newspaper include this article? _____

_____

Focus 2: Apostrophes

The poor apostrophe is probably the most misused punctuation mark – either it isn't there when it's needed or it's put into places where it doesn't belong. There are examples everywhere you look. Here's a greengrocer who just can't get it right!

Remember – an apostrophe is used in two main ways:

- **Contraction** – one or more letters has or have been missed out.
  For example, 'isn't' means 'is not' – the 'o' has been dropped.
- **Possession** – something belongs to something else.
  For example, the dog's tail – the dog owns, or possesses, the tail.

> Its spring — come in and buy spring vegetables today!
> *(It's (It is) spring, he means)*
>
> Carrot's on special
> *(just one carrot, then?)*
>
> New potato's and kumara
> *(one potato's what???)*
>
> Get you're gourmet greens here
> *(Get you are greens...?)*

A few things to remember …

Contraction

Writers use contractions to make their writing less formal. Contractions can make the words seem more like conversation. When you contract two words in your own writing, always remember to put the apostrophe in the right place.

Tom does not like it when his brother is mean to him.
Tom doesn't like it when his brother's mean to him.

Possessive pronouns

Possessive pronouns are:

mine, yours, his, hers, its, ours, yours, theirs.

None of these needs an apostrophe.

Only 'its' seems to cause problems for students. Just remember, if you can use 'it is' or 'it has' instead, then an apostrophe is required. For example:

It's a long way to the beach. Even the dog will need to take its lunch along.

You do:

1 As this is a bit of an issue, here's an exercise for you to test yourself. Read this short passage and put in all the necessary apostrophes. Use a bright felt pen and only put one in when you *know* it is needed.

> Susan stood at the edge of the lake watching the windsurfers. Ill never be able to do that she thought to herself.
> 'Dad, I dont want to do this,' she said to her father, standing beside her.
> 'Im sure youll be fine once you get started,' he reassured her, 'its easy, really it is.'
> One windsurfers sail suddenly keeled over and he slipped off his board into the murky water. Watching him claw his way back to the boards surface with great difficulty, Susan sighed and picked up her sisters wetsuit. Better get it over with, Dad wasnt going to give up that easily.

2 You might try rewriting the greengrocer's sign too.

ISBN 9780170195935

Week _____ Date for completion _____

Parent's sig. _____ Teacher's sig. _____

Focus 1: Visual close reading

ROCKET FUEL FOR YOUR CAREER!

Careers in retail rock! If you don't want to be stuck behind a desk all day in a boring office environment doing the same thing over and over again… choose retail for a future that's going places. Why retail?

Retail offers career paths, fast progression and promotion and great job opportunities.

Retail has variety – positions include Visual Merchandiser, Buyer, Account Manager, Regional Manager, Marketing Manager, Financial Controller, Managing Director and loads more.

Retail is fun! Fast-paced, funky products, cool colleagues, wicked high-energy atmosphere and great money!

NZQA qualifications available nationwide while working full-time and getting full-pay. No exams, no fees and no student loan! Go to www.retailito.org.nz for information on retail qualifications.

WHY RETAIL?
WHY NOT!
www.rwr.co.nz

Read the advertisement through carefully and highlight/annotate the **layout** elements of a visual text.

Then look for as many examples of **verbal techniques** and **visual techniques** as you can possibly find. Make sure you do this tidily. Do not ruin your ability to see the overall image.

Layout
- Headline
- Image
- Body copy
- Background
- Logo/slogan

Visual techniques
Point of contrast
Bold lettering
Logos

Verbal techniques
Tone of language
Play on words
Repetition
Use of adjectives for effect
Personal pronouns
Alliteration
Rhetorical question
Contractions

ISBN 9780170195935

Now you have spent some time analysing the advertisement, answer the questions that follow.

1 a Who/what is being advertised (product/service)?

 b Who is being targeted (audience)?

 c What is the overall message we are intended to get from the text (message)?

2 Clearly explain the connection between the background graphic and the rest of the advertisement.

3 How does the language of this article aim to reach the teenage market? Use examples from the text in your answer.

4 Why is the word 'retail' used so many times?

5 What is the significance of the logos on the right-hand side of the advertisement?

6 Why have most of these logos been put on a plain white background?

7 At the bottom of the advertisement you are given a website, www.rwr.co.nz. Look carefully through the rest of the advertisement to find out what the 'rwr' stands for.

Focus 2: Pronouns in advertising

Where will you need to be aware of pronouns?

In your study of English you will be asked to talk about pronouns, directly or indirectly, in a variety of circumstances. You may be tackling a close reading exercise, or analysing a poem or advertisement or perhaps preparing a speech.
 Your task may be to explain why a writer has employed a pronoun. Take advertising for example:

You need cool walls. Get your icy bricks today. Use of 'you', 'your' is trying to involve the audience, the potential buyer, by addressing them directly.

We're all in this together. Here the advertiser of a welfare organisation wants to get the audience to feel part of the solution, involvement of a different kind.

You do:

Find five examples of TV or magazine advertisements that feature the following pronouns. For each quote the relevant phrase and explain why the advertiser is using these pronouns.

1 you, yours

2 I, me, mine

3 they, them, their

4 he, she

5 we, our

ISBN 9780170195935

Week _____ Date for completion _____

Parent's sig. _____ Teacher's sig. _____

Focus 1: Understanding poetry

Do you remember the process to analysing a poem?

Step 1: Read – preferably aloud.
Step 2: Reread quietly, take in main ideas.
Step 3: Use dictionary to help you with difficult vocabulary.
Step 4: Read again.
Step 5: Highlight poetic techniques.
Step 6: Discuss as a class/in pairs.
Step 7: Now you have all the information, reread the poem. Enjoy it!
Step 8: Answer any questions that follow.

You will need to look up the highlighted words in order to fully understand this poem. Use the arrows to help you with your annotation.

- tethered
- senescent
- sodden
- shackled
- recast
- galley
- surly

Locate the following techniques by underlining and annotating beside the poem.

- Personification
- Alliteration
- Onomatopoeia
- Repetition
- Metaphor

NB: If you get stuck, you might want to do the activity at the bottom of page 29 first.

Dinghy at the Water's Edge

Tethered at the salt water's edge
This senescent hull has nowhere now
To go. All that's left of her
Is a bared wooden keel; the rotted floor

Is back with the sea. Each day
The sliding tide laps up to lick
And lick again long sodden remains,
And whispering, returns to the belly

Of the harbour. Each night the same.
A fisherman I watched used once
To row her out. No longer though, for
She lies shackled on soft mangrove mud.

When boys see her they slosh to her
There. Boarding, they recast her to sea
In their game. She is a galley and they
Surly sea men guiding her knowingly to shore.

by John Geraets

Answer the following questions:

1   Using words/phrases from the poem, describe the dinghy in the poem.

_____

_____

_____

_____

2   The poet uses two words to describe how the dinghy is anchored in the mangroves. Which words are they? For
    each word decide whether it has a positive or negative tone.

First word: _____   Tone: _____

Second word: _____   Tone: _____

3   To what features of the sea is the poet alluding with the lines 'The sliding tide laps up to lick / and lick again ...'?

_____

_____

_____

4   How do you know that the poet has watched this dinghy for many years?

_____

_____

_____

_____

5   In the last stanza the poet uses the word 'game'. What is the game and who is playing it?

_____

_____

_____

_____

_____

Focus 2: Poetry recap

Time to put your thinking caps on. Match the terms, definitions and examples below using the grid to record
your answers.

Term	Definition	Example
1 ALLITERATION	(a) When a word, line or verse is repeated several times in the poem.	(i) Her eyes shone like diamonds.
2 METAPHOR	(b) When the word that is being used sounds like the action it is describing.	(ii) Silly Sally sat sadly upon the satin sheets.
3 SIMILE	(c) Giving a non-human object human characteristics.	(iii) The sea moaned, moaned, moaned.
4 REPETITION	(d) Saying that something *is* something else.	(iv) And all the trees have silver skirts.
5 ONOMATOPOEIA	(e) Saying something is like something else – always use 'like' or 'as'.	(v) I've got a dog as thin as a rail, He's got fleas all over his tail.
6 RHYME	(f) The repetition of sounds at the beginning of a group of words.	(vi) The wind was a whip that cracked over our heads.
7 PERSONIFICATION	(g) When the ends of the words sound the same.	(vii) We cursed the horrible six-inch sludge!

Term	1	2	3	4	5	6	7
Definition							
Example							

ISBN 9780170195935

UNIT 8

Week _____ Date for completion _____

Parent's sig. _____ Teacher's sig. _____

HINT FOR SUCCESS
Stuck for ideas for a formal essay topic? Remember, you have other school subjects to provide you with information. Many essay topics could incorporate information you have learnt in Science, Geography or PE.

Focus 1: Formal writing – wind energy: yes or no?

Writing a formal essay

The introduction will:

- state the topic
- state your point of view (which side of the argument you are presenting)
- give the three main ideas you will use
- be interesting and convincing.

The body of the essay will:

- have no fewer than three ideas in three separate paragraphs.

All good paragraphs should have:

- a topic sentence that states the idea
- an explanation saying in more detail what you meant in your topic sentence
- evidence that supports your explanation with an effective example. Anecdote, statistic, quotation, …
- a concluding connection to the topic.

The conclusion of the essay will:

- restate the main points of the essay
- reinforce the writer's attitude without giving any new information
- end with a strong, thought-provoking statement or question.

Essentials:

- correct spelling
- correct paragraphing
- correct use of punctuation

Ideals:

- expressive vocabulary
- good organisation or structure
- great ideas

Don't forget:
Try to imagine your essay is the last thing that the person making the final decision on your issue will read and it should therefore persuade them to agree with your opinion.

If you need more guidance on writing a formal essay, refer to chapter 6 of your *How to …* textbook.

Tricks of the trade:

- use a dictionary
- use a thesaurus
- use a spell checker (machine and person)
- use an editor
- and for those elusive ideas – the brainstorm!

You do:

Your task is to write a formal essay on the topic:

Wind energy is the way of the future.

To complete this task effectively you will need to visit the Meridian Energy website, www.meridianenergy.co.nz. Here you will find links to information about how Meridian is developing wind energy in New Zealand. This should help you with the content of the essay.

Below is a collection of points that have been compiled to help you with your initial thinking and planning. You can use them to help you process the information from Meridian. Of course you may like to widen your search while you are on the Internet.

Feel free to argue whichever side of the issue you like.

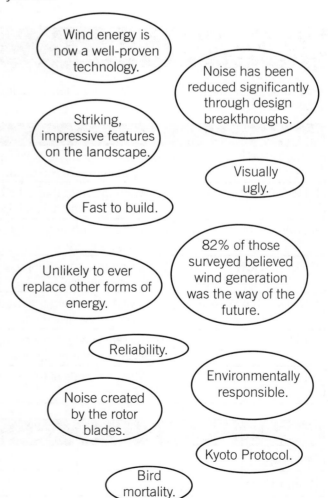

Wind energy is now a well-proven technology.

Noise has been reduced significantly through design breakthroughs.

Striking, impressive features on the landscape.

Visually ugly.

Fast to build.

Unlikely to ever replace other forms of energy.

82% of those surveyed believed wind generation was the way of the future.

Reliability.

Environmentally responsible.

Noise created by the rotor blades.

Kyoto Protocol.

Bird mortality.

ISBN 9780170195935

We have left you some space for planning. Write the final copy of your essay in the back of this book.

_____
_____
_____
_____
_____
_____
_____

Focus 2: Colloquial language and slang

Colloquial

Colloquial language is the ordinary, everyday speech of a particular place and time period. It is informal, casual and conversational. It's also acceptable enough for you to use with your parents and possibly your grandparents. In these first years of the twenty-first century, informal language is changing all of the time but there are some examples that are easy to recognise. Much that is colloquial is a shortened version of existing words:

> barbie – barbecue
> cabbie – cab driver, taxi driver
> veggies – vegetables
> boardies – board shorts

Two words are often collapsed into one as we speak more rapidly than we write. 'I have' becomes 'I've' and 'I am' becomes 'I'm'.

Sometimes words are used in new ways. It has been acceptable to use 'cool' to mean good as well as quite cold for some time. Also, guy can mean a man, youth, boy, or even a girl.

Newspaper columnists who write human-interest columns and novelists who want to give their characters natural-sounding conversations use colloquial language. Just try to avoid using colloquialisms in your formal writing.

Slang

Slang is informal, made-up language that is found in a particular place at a particular time. Each generation formulates its own slang and these words are usually 'passing phases'. People don't tend to use the words 'fab' and 'groovy' now to express positive feelings about something. Both words were common among teenagers in the 1960s.

Slang is often used to promote a 'hip' or 'cool' image. It is usually created or adopted by a certain group of people, for example, surfers or teenagers, then copied by others and may later be accepted into colloquial, spoken language. Some examples are 'cool', 'chick', 'dude' and 'nerd'.

Use of slang is often deemed undignified but at the time may be humorous and vivid. For instance if a teenager tells another teenager that he will get the money from his 'old man', this is acceptable. However, if he tells his principal that he'll get the money from his 'old man', this is insulting and inappropriate.

Slang is unacceptable in most situations you will be in as part of your education but it is important to be able to recognise what is slang – and then usually avoid it!

You do:

See how many words you can find that mean the words in the following list. Look for colloquial and slang examples. Ask your grandparents and parents for the colloquial or slang words used in their day and add ones that your generation uses today.

	Grandparents	Parents	Today
Girl			
Boy			
Child			
School bus			
Outing			
Dad			
Mum			
Friend			
Good			
Horrible			
Silly			

ISBN 9780170195935

UNIT 9

Focus 1: Creative writing

The aim of practising writing skills is to express yourself in a simple, accurate and interesting manner. Let's remind ourselves about the process of writing a successful piece of narrative writing.

Narrative recap

Structure
Think about what structure you are going to use. You will need to set the scene, introduce the characters, describe the event/problem, the climax and resolution. The order you do this in helps to keep your story original.

Conflict
Conflict is the element in the story that will keep the audience interested. It may be between:
- a character and what is happening
- a character and someone else in the story
- a character and their conscience
- a character and the environment.

Characters
Most stories will have a character in a dilemma. Your character might be in:
- a crisis
- a place new to them
- an unusual circumstance
- conflict with another character.

Credible plot
Remember that if the character and the situation are familiar and interesting to you, you will be that much more successful in convincing your reader. And it's easier to get started if you base your imaginings on things you know something about.

Ready to write?
Work through the following steps to help you achieve a completed piece of writing:
1 Developing ideas
2 Composing a draft
3 Getting feedback and comments from others
4 Revising the draft by expanding ideas, clarifying meaning, reorganising
5 Editing
6 Presenting the finished work.

Go to page 103 of *How to …* if you need more guidance.

Below is a writing starter on which to base a piece of narrative writing.
Read it carefully and *without* talking to anyone else complete a brainstorm in the space provided below.

Take the time to brainstorm your ideas. Jotting down spontaneous ideas, key words and phrases will help you see if you have enough ideas and allow you to order your thoughts.

> I lay on my bed, staring at the ceiling, my entire body quaking with fear and adrenaline. What had I done? Why had I done it? I only know that I got a great sense of excitement from it. My breathing slowed to its normal rate, and I looked at the prized object clasped in my desperate childish fingers. ...

_____

_____

_____

_____

_____

_____

Now you have had a chance to think about your story, write your piece. Write the final copy of your story in the back of this book.

ISBN 9780170195935

Duz spelnk matr?

Short answer: Yes.

Long answer: You will not get far in school or in the competitive employment world if you cannot write coherent English with reasonably correct spelling. There will always be really hard words – that's where dictionaries help – but you must make every effort to spell well.

There are patterns in English, despite all the irregularities. We cannot do a lot of work here, but look at these examples:

1 When a word ends in 'y', it usually changes to 'i' before adding any ending:

story – stories
pity – pitiful
rely – reliable

Add an ending to these words:

lady   – _____

army   – _____

glory – _____

supply – _____

pretty – _____

fury   – _____

2 Many words use the 'le' ending.
Add to these lists:

...ble	...ple	...tle
table	apple	battle
impossible	example	cattle
capable	principle	little
double	sample	title
*	*	*
*	*	*
*	*	*

However, there will always be exceptions:

sandal, scandal, hospital, pistol, pupil, cannibal, rebel

Some things you just have to learn.

You do:

Here is a list of words that are often spelt incorrectly.
Write them correctly in the space provided. Then use a dictionary to see if you are right.

rythm   _____

parliment   _____

libary   _____

principul   _____

beatiful   _____

anoyed   _____

morgage   _____

neccessary _____

behavior   _____

disapoint   _____

dissapear   _____

brekfast   _____

feild   _____

belive   _____

occassion   _____

vegitable   _____

wisper   _____

colum   _____

asignment   _____

fulfill   _____

In the accompanying textbook we talked about the differences between American and British spellings. Look at the list below and decide which is the commonly used spelling in New Zealand.

New Zealand English tends to follow British English spelling rules. Write the New Zealand English version of these words in the spaces provided:

American spelling	Usual New Zealand spelling
color	
labor	
aluminum	
plow	
favorite	
criticize	
analyze	
center	
theater	
skillful	
enrollment	
catalog	
dialog	
analog	
aging	
judgment	
defense	
jewelry	
pajamas	

ISBN 9780170195935

Week _____ Date for completion _____

Parent's sig. _____ Teacher's sig. _____

HINT FOR SUCCESS
Try to answer all the questions when answering a close reading. You never know, you might just stumble across the right answer!

Focus 1: Written close reading

By now you will have done some work honing your close reading skills. We assume you have worked through the exercises in the *How to …* textbook and Unit 5 of this book. Go back to either for a recap on how to approach close reading of a written text.

Read the passage below and answer the questions that follow.

> The driver ants are carnivorous and nomadic. From time to time the army stops its march and when this happens, it disappears into various hiding places while scouts are sent out to explore the countryside. The information the scouts bring back helps them map their route. Once the route is decided, the order is given and <u>the earth belches ants</u>. A million pour out and form into line, roughly five abreast, and the advance begins. This is a very disciplined march. Along the ranks the big-headed soldiers, the officers, run directing the march, frequently meeting in little groups for apparent discussions. 5
>
> Nothing living will stop that column. Anything in its path is destroyed; even the gigantic python that can swallow a deer is killed and eaten if it does not get out of the way.
>
> A house is invaded silently, generally at night. Everything in that house that lives is killed. Before morning the ants will leave and the owner can return to find a house that is clean and all vermin, from rats to bugs, is wiped out — as also will be his poultry and stock if it is not set free — but food, other than meat, will be untouched. 10
>
> A man caught asleep is covered by the driver ants who do him no harm at all until presumably a signal is given. Then, all attack simultaneously. Each ant plunges in its pincers and pulls until the portion of flesh it has grasped comes out. That pincer grip never relaxes, even in death. 15
>
> The natives of the area, who might be miles away from medical help, put this tenacity of the ants to good use. When they have wounds that need to be stitched, they use the pincers of the driver ants to bind the edges together. It is a tricky job, but the ant is made to bite so that one pincer is on the one side of the cut and the other pincer on the other side. The closing pincers hold the edges of the wounds together and the ant's body is then cut off. It is most effective surgery. 20

1 The earth belches ants (line 4) means:

    a The ants go up in smoke.   c The earth is burping.

    b The ants pour out of the ground.   d The ants are burping.   a   b   c   d

2 The ants like to eat meat. Find ONE word in the passage that means they eat meat. _____

3 Identify TWO things mentioned in the passage that the driver ants would eat.

    i _____ ii _____

4 The ants live in one area only. Is this statement true or false? _____

5 Find a quotation from the passage that supports your answer for Question 4.

_____

6 Explain in your own words the role the scouts play.

_____

_____

7 Do the ants bite a person immediately if they find him asleep? Give evidence from the text to support your answer.

_____

_____

8 What does the word 'vermin', as used in line 11, mean? _____

9 Replace 'simultaneously' (line 15) with a word/phrase that has the same meaning. _____

10 Explain in your own words how the writer extends the metaphor that compares the driver ants with an army.

_____

_____

_____

_____

ISBN 9780170195935

Focus 2: Homonyms and homophones

Homonyms

Homonyms are words spelt and pronounced in an identical way, but they have different meanings and functions. Cryptic crosswords use them a lot.

The **bat** flew into the cave.   His cricket **bat** was brand new.   He will **bat** first for his team.

The first two sentences have the noun *bat*, but meaning different things, and the third is the verb *to bat*.

Here's a little exercise – fill in the gap in each section with the same word.

1   The dog has a loud _____.
    The _____ of the tree showed its age.

2   Judges should always try to be _____.
    There was plenty to buy at the _____.

3   He works for a retail _____.
    Her parents are _____, but fair.

4   The _____ are causing pollution.
    She _____ when she's angry.

5   Not a _____ could be heard.
    He is of _____ mind and body.

6   The cargo was in the _____ of the ship.
    _____ my hand while we cross the road.

7   He is stuck in a traffic _____.
    Strawberry _____ is delicious on toast.
    Be careful not to _____ the paper in the printer.

Homophones

Homophones are words that are pronounced in the same way, but differ in spelling and meaning. They are confusing words and often result in spelling errors.
For example:

We talk **aloud**.
We are **allowed** to go.

He **threw** the ball **through** the hoop.

He was **too** tired to play **two** matches.

We **pray** for peace.
The lion caught its **prey**.

The car has a flat **tyre**.
The illness causes him to **tire**.

She has a small **waist**.
Do not **waste** your money.

The **principals** have high **principles**.

We buy school **stationery**.
The vehicle is **stationary**.

Show you understand the meaning of each of the following sets of homophones by writing your own sentences.

1   mussel/muscle
    _____
    _____

2   peace/piece
    _____
    _____

3   rap/wrap
    _____
    _____

4   whether/weather
    _____
    _____

5   site/cite/sight
    _____
    _____

> In Unit 9 we asked you to learn the spelling of some commonly misspelt words. Get a parent, sibling or friend to test you on your ability to still remember these words.

You may be wondering why you are being reminded about homophones. One very good reason is that you are probably using the computer spell-checker to check the accuracy of your writing. The problem many students encounter with computer spell-checkers is that they cannot choose the correct word for meaning, only for spelling. It is up to you to choose wisely.

   Look at the following passage – a computer spell-checker would not recognise any errors. Hopefully you do. Rewrite it below correctly.

   Wee saw a sale at see. It seamed to bee hour principle's lit till craft but in thyme wee sore it was won bee longing to an udder person.

_____
_____
_____

ISBN 9780170195935

Week _____ Date for completion _____

Parent's sig. _____ Teacher's sig. _____

Focus 1: Creating character notes

You will be asked to write about the main characters in text you study. It will be a lot easier to do this if you have first prepared some notes. Try the method below using the text you are currently studying in class.

What he/she looks like (5 min)

-
-
-
-
-
-

Something interesting the character says (5min)

Character drawing

What his/her problems are (5 min)

-
-
-
-
-
-

Describe his/her personality (5 min)

-
-
-
-
-
-

Use the information you have listed here to write a paragraph about the character. We have left you some space for planning. Write the final copy of your essay in the back of this book.

_____
_____
_____
_____

ISBN 9780170195935

Focus 2: Paragraphing

A paragraph is formed from a group of sentences that have something in common; when put together they are linked as one part of an argument or the unfolding of a story.

You will often be reminded to use paragraphs effectively in your essay writing, keeping a single idea to a paragraph. Using paragraphs well helps to structure your essay in a logical order.

When you are writing creatively you need to recognise there are other places you need to use paragraphs too.

New paragraph for a change of speaker

When writing dialogue, it is essential to begin a new paragraph every time one person begins to speak. This lets the reader know who is speaking.

New paragraph for the passing of time

When an important passage of time has occurred, you begin a new paragraph.

New paragraph for a change of place

Characters in a story often move from one place to another. Whether or not a new paragraph is required depends upon how much the move affects the development of the story.

New paragraph for a new person

A new paragraph is usually required to introduce a person into a story. In some stories, a character is 'on stage' all the time; in others he or she may not be referred to for a few paragraphs. When the character returns to the story, a new paragraph is required only if he or she is important to the development of the plot.

> When you read anything, whether it is a textbook for Geography, a novel for English, a magazine article or a column in a newspaper, stop and look at the way the paragraphs are organised to make it easy for you to follow the writing and its ideas.

You do:

Read the passage below carefully. For each of the paragraphs say why the writer has started a new paragraph here.

1. Stanley was asleep on the sofa in the living room in the middle of a hot summer afternoon. His head rested comfortably on his Mum's best cushion and his feet draped inelegantly over the sofa arm, hanging just above his cricket shoes.

2. The front door slammed open and then, with even more force, shut.

3. 'Stanley!' came the shrill voice of his grandmother. 'Stanley, where are you? I need you, right now!!!'

4. The air in the living room around Stanley vibrated as the door swung open and Gran swept in. She might be small but she knew how to make an entrance. Her pink sunhat, purple flowered dress and white 'comfy' sandals filled Stanley's vision as he forced his eyes open.

5. 'Ouch, don't pinch me,' he said, 'I'm awake already. I'm awake, what is it?' Stanley sat up and shook his head to clear it of the pleasant dream he'd been having about scoring the winning runs.

6. Gran by now was in the armchair removing her sandals but not her hat. She liked to think it gave her an added air of authority. 'We've got a problem, Stan,' she said.

1 _____

2 _____

3 _____

4 _____

5 _____

6 _____

ISBN 9780170195935

Week ＿＿＿＿＿＿ Date for completion ＿＿＿＿＿＿＿

Parent's sig. ＿＿＿＿＿＿ Teacher's sig. ＿＿＿＿＿＿

HINT FOR SUCCESS
Find new words: use a thesaurus to help liven up your writing.

Focus 1: Poetry writing – Diamantes

A Diamante is a poem or stanza of seven lines that follows a strict structure.

Light
limpid, keen
dazzling, sparkling, beaming
clarity, crystal, ebony, mystery
shrouding, obscuring, enveloping
shadowy, soft
Dark.

Line length	Content or purpose	Words
1 One word	names subject	noun
2 Two words	describes the subject in line 1	adjectives
3 Three words	describes the subject in line 1	participles (-ing, -ed)
4 Four words	first two relate to line 1 subject; second two relate to line 7 subject	nouns
5 Three words	describe the subject in line 7	participles (-ing, -ed)
6 Two words	describe the subject in line 7	adjectives
7 One word	names a subject that is the antonym of the line 1 subject	noun

Here are some more examples.

Square
symmetrical, conventional
shaping, measuring, balancing
boxes, rooms, clocks, halos
encircling, circumnavigating, enclosing
round, continuous
Circle

Use different-coloured highlighters to show the two parts of each poem.

Winter
rainy, cold
skiing, skating, sledding
mountains, wind, breeze, ocean
swimming, surfing, scuba diving
sunny, hot
Summer

Teenager
powerful, noisy
dancing, dating, consuming
explosion, energetic, maturity, senility
working, earning, saving
quiet, peaceful
Old-ager

Winter
frosty, bright
skiing, snowball fighting, sledding
icicles, snowflakes, vacation, family
swimming, sun tanning, sweltering
hot, sunny
Summer

Dreams
subconscious, imaginary
sleeping, wishing, thinking
fantasy, actuality, vision, genuine
being, seeing, knowing,
authentic, factual
Reality

You do:

Draft your own Diamante poem and copy your final version on to the lines provided.

You may have an idea of something that will work already but if not, why not use one of our suggestions:

- starting schoolboy and finishing schoolgirl
- starting Mum and ending Dad
- starting Mum and ending Grandma/Nana
- starting city and ending country.

＿＿＿＿＿＿＿＿＿＿＿＿

＿＿＿＿＿＿＿＿＿＿＿＿

＿＿＿＿＿＿＿＿＿＿＿＿

＿＿＿＿＿＿＿＿＿＿＿＿

＿＿＿＿＿＿＿＿＿＿＿＿

ISBN 9780170195935

Focus 2: Adjectives

We all know that an adjective is a describing word. Adjectives add meaning to a noun or a pronoun; they give us more information about a word. Adjectives also add interest and colour to sentences by giving more detailed information.

For example:

A bird flew across the sky.

A bright, blue bird flew across the sun-streaked sky.   *What sort of bird? What sort of sky?*

Adjectives add interest and colour to sentences. Using them carefully will improve your own writing, but it's important not to overuse them. Read this short extract from Lewis Carroll's *Alice in Wonderland* in which he uses a few well-chosen adjectives:

> '... she came upon a low curtain she had not noticed before, and behind it was a little door about fifteen inches high: she tried the little golden key in the lock, and to her great delight it fitted!
> Alice opened the door and found that it led into a small passage, not much larger than a rat-hole: she knelt down and looked along the passage into the loveliest garden you ever saw. How she longed to get out of that dark hall, and wander about among those beds of bright flowers and those cool fountains.'

You may well be asked to identify adjectives, but you also have to explain why a writer has chosen the particular ones. Notice how most of these adjectives tend to fall into groups that support the impressions Carroll is trying to put across to his reader.

You do:

Highlight the adjectives in the extract from *Alice in Wonderland* (above) and then explain what qualities the writer is focusing on by using these words.

_____

_____

_____

You do:

Adjectives are used a great deal in advertising. You will be asked to identify and explain them and you may well be asked to select some for advertisements of your own. Highlight all the adjectives you can see in these advertisements. Under each one say what it is about the product that the adjectives focus on. The first is done for you as an example.

Packed with only the finest, freshest ingredients and triple concentrated for maximum flavour, Leggo's Tomato Paste will bring out the very best in your favourite dishes.

Focus: quality and taste

Nutra-Life Hi-Omega Flaxseed Oil is 100% pure High-Omega 3 Flaxseed Oil, cold-pressed from special organically grown whole flaxseed. Nutra-Life Hi-Omega Flaxseed Oil helps to maintain circulation and healthy vibrant skin.

Germ-X is an instant waterless hand sanitiser that kills 99.99% of common harmful germs and bacteria that can make you sick. It works in as little as 15 seconds, leaving your hands feeling clean, pleasant smelling and moisturised with vitamin E. Germ-X, it pays you to keep it on hand.

Focus: _____

Focus: _____

Have soft, smooth, glowing skin all year round when you apply JOHNSON'S Holiday Skin every day. This ground-breaking new formula moisturises your skin while building a light natural-looking tan. JOHNSON'S Holiday Skin hydrates the skin for all-day moisturisation, while a small amount of self tan builds a natural-looking golden colour, without the fuss and smell of self-tanning lotions. Now you can have glowing skin all year round.

Focus: _____

39

ISBN 9780170195935

Week _____ Date for completion _____

Parent's sig. _____ Teacher's sig. _____

Focus 1: Analyse a review

THE GOOD, THE BAD AND THE DUSTY

For this review, we tried to ask all our friends who'd been to the event to write their intelligent thoughts down to help us get a well rounded perspective of experiences at Rhythm and Vines. Unfortunately their thoughts were not very intelligent and by the time we censored all the scandalous references about chicks, booze and other naughties, we were left with comments about the dust. And yes, Rhythm and Vines was very dusty and it seems it has settled in many memories as a major player of the event. What I couldn't believe was the property owners wanted to turn their beautiful landscape into a potential mud hole … could they not have planted grass? Perhaps the decision to extend the party to 10,000 punters was such a last minute decision that they just enlisted the help of a bulldozer. I guess the dust did add a 'smokey' atmosphere. However by the end of the night I looked like a dirty, smelly tramp. Dust aside, the venue was fairly well arranged. As an R&V old timer, I was kind of bummed that the intimacy of previous years was lost to a 'show ground' affair. The space was immense and included a water slide, food and bev stands and possibly the best toilets I've ever experienced at an outdoor event. Seriously, the toilets were awesome. They flushed. And loo paper was always well stocked. Not to keep talking about the loos or anything, but when are the chicks going to learn that they don't have to stand in ridiculous lines or squat in the vines in public view. Smart people found alternative entrances, used the boy's loos or found the secret toilets scattered around the venue that no one seemed to know about. They were like toilet heaven.

Now to more serious things … the music and vibe. The energy of the event was immense. Everyone was excited and on big adventures. Highlights for me were Kors, Sola Rosa, Freq Nasty, Pitch Black and Fat Freddy's. The general vibe though seemed to be that people were craving a few more dancey dancey acts. Many commented that the music was too mellow. Fortunately some were lucky enough to stumble across DJ Phully who was playing

to almost no one during the Fat Freddy's gig. I caught his last two tracks and was like, 'this guy is awesome', and then he finished. To be absolutely honest I was so confused between the two stages and about where I should be going and losing friends that I never really settled until Pitch Black at 4.30 in the morning. The great thing about having one stage like previous years, is that there is never that confusion and chaos. Thank God for those beautiful Birch trees that became the meeting point for many lost partiers.

At about 3am, Gizzy got incredibly cold. It seemed that most people were not prepared for the night temperatures as it plummeted below comfort level for those who had lost their tops or who had worn hot pants and singlets to cope with the day time heat. All I remember is shivering chicks and guys who had found random bits of material or signage lying around, covering themselves and heading for their cars. Bummer, they missed the best bit.

There is nothing more beautiful than watching the sun disappear behind the cornfields and then reappear above the vines. By sunrise, the few people who were left, grabbed their little tents and headed for the small stage to take in the last act, watch the sunrise, chill out and reflect upon their night. It was certainly a huge event and maybe I'm just a Gemini so easily confused when presented with two stages. I think most people absolutely loved it and if a big party's your thing for New Years, check it out next year as it will be even bigger.

Oh yeah, was it just me or did they have technical problems before the countdown? New Years came in late … an auspicious omen perhaps?

1   Look at the tone created in this review. What does it suggest about

    a   the author? _____

    b   the audience? _____

2   Review titles are often catchy. Explain what is catchy about this one. (Clue: Ask your parents!)

    _____

    _____

3   Choose two different-coloured highlighters and highlight the positive things and then the negative things that have been talked about in this review.

4   Give an example of where each of the following techniques have been used in the text. Underline each and annotate using the corresponding letter.

    a   Lively language to entertain and inform.

    b   Vocabulary includes words more commonly seen in print than heard in everyday speech.

    c   Mixes this with colloquial terms.

    d   Contractions to create chatty tone.

    e   Emotive words to convey attitudes/judgements.

    f   Present tense to give sense of immediacy.

    g   Information and comments on character/actors/setting/techniques/direction/genre.

    h   Development of a point of view from which the reviewer judges the work.

    i   Honesty, balance, supporting information.

ISBN 9780170195935

5   This review may be slightly different to others you would have read because it is about a one-off event. Give two reasons why this review would have been included for publication in a magazine.

_____

_____

Focus 2: How to write ... a film review

Film reviews are a wonderful way of evaluating a film. Regardless of the type of film or the age of the film, film reviews allow people to determine whether or not they think they might like a film before seeing it.

Your job this week is to write a review for one of the following:

- A film you are going to see at the theatre (so as you can watch carefully and jot down some quick notes immediately after the session).
- A DVD you choose for over the weekend.
- A film that you will watch on one of the television channels.

Note: Do not choose a film you have seen already, even if it was only last week. It is important that the film you work with has been watched critically, not just for leisure.

When writing a film review, there are several different guidelines to follow. Carefully read the information below before you begin your review.

Go back to chapter 7 of the *How to ...* text and reread the appropriate pages on writing reviews.

Basic elements

The following outline offers the basic elements that should be found in any good film review. Not all of the elements listed below may be applicable to all films, however these criteria provide a general overview for all components that should be included in a basic film review.

Title of review
Name of film being reviewed
Date of when film was reviewed
Name of author/reviewer
Intended audience (children, teenagers, young adults, adults)
Rating (G, PG, PG-13, M, R)
Genre of film (comedy, drama, action, adventure, horror, thriller)
Opening date/year of release
Name of producer
Length of film
Actors/actresses in film
– Are the characters in the film easy to understand?
– Quality of acting
Sound track/music
Give a brief summary of the plot but do not spoil the ending
Is the movie easy to follow?
Compare to other films
Director – what other films has this director done?
Overall rating

A generic outline

This outline will help you get going. Assume you are writing for your classmates. Your audience will determine the style, structure and length of your review.

Title	Catchy, you can play with words to make it funny or different.
Para 1	Opening paragraph – can start to summarise film and give early suggestions about your general review of it.
Para 2	Start or continue summary of film; don't give details about the end or else no one will go and see the film!
Paras 3–4	Positive things you thought about the film. What did you like? Why?
Paras 5–6	Negative things you thought about the film. What did you not like? Why?
Para 7	Characterisation – talk about the characters. Did you like them? Did the actors play them well? Will certain audience members not like certain characters? Why not?
Para 8	Final comments – general comments that summarise your view of the film. You may want to say something inspiring to get the reader to want to go out and see the film.
Rating	At the end you could give your film a star rating to indicate your overall opinion of the product.

Below are some words/phrases commonly used in film reviews that you might want to use in your own reviews.

spectacular visual effects, excessive violence, breathtaking, evocative, mood, atmosphere, poorly, unsuccessful, detail, scenery, irresistible, perfect, plot, this movie has been compared to ... because ... wonderful, hilarious, momentum, unexpected plot twists, unbelievable, phenomenal, hype, suspense, disappointing, confused, fake, imitation, genre, unoriginal, typical, thrilled, was a very moving portrayal, quality of the film, I was impressed by, credible, cliché, a mixture of, classic, captivating.

Movie reviews are an excellent way of communicating information about different types of movie. The next time you decide to pay $9 to go see a movie or $5 to rent one, read a review and see if you really want to pay for it.

ISBN 9780170195935

Focus 1: Making a visual image

Part of being able to analyse an image is being able to incorporate the techniques commonly used by professional designers into your own work. Being able to use these techniques for a purposeful effect yourself means you can then reflect on why the professionals would use them.

New Zealand Post is frequently updating the look of its stamps. We are going to give you a chance to design a stamp which reflects/illustrates a place or concept that is significant to you about your own country.

You may pick any conventional stamp shape or size, although we suggest you enlarge the stamp to make it easier for you to work with.

Try and make your stamp look as professional as possible. Do not forget to include: a white border, a money 'amount', and the words 'New Zealand'.

Keep the following things in mind.

Let's recap ...

- Plan the layout, size, shape, colours of the static image.
- Decide on symbols/main images.
- Carefully choose the words to appear on the static image.
- Use materials that work well for the message.
- Use tools (ruler, set square, good scissors, photocopier, and so on) if you need to.

How are you going to incorporate visual techniques?

Colour
Contrast
Font (style and size)
Layout
Point of impact
Illustration/graphic
Unusual images
Symbols

What style is your stamp going to be?

Photographic
Collage
Modern
Sketched
Symbolic

What technology are you going to use?

Travel brochures
Magazines
Felts
Paint
Computer graphics

Go back to chapter 14 of your *How to ...* book to look at more ideas on style and illustrations.

Once you have completed your postage stamp we suggest you glue it into the inside back cover of this book. Then answer the following questions.

1   Describe where, and explain why you chose the **colours** that you did.

_____
_____
_____

2   Choice of font is an important part of visual work. Describe clearly the **lettering** style(s) you used and explain why you chose it/them.

_____
_____
_____

3   List each **visual feature** that you used and explain why it suited your image, the effect it had and how it might appeal to users.

_____
_____
_____

4   Describe clearly any areas of **contrast** you used in your image and explain the effect you were hoping to achieve. Border? Heading? Reverse print?

_____
_____
_____

ISBN 9780170195935

5   Describe the **layout** of your image and explain the reasons behind your choices. For instance, why have you chosen to put your pictures where you have?

_____

_____

_____

6   What is the **dominant visual feature** of your image? What was the effect you were trying to achieve?

_____

_____

_____

7   Describe any **features of your image that you would want to repeat** next time and explain clearly why you thought they worked.

_____

_____

_____

_____

8   **Things can always be improved**. Look critically at your image and describe any feature you would change if you repeated this exercise, explaining how you think this would improve your image.

_____

_____

_____

_____

Focus 2: Visual and verbal techniques

It is important for you to learn the basic verbal and visual techniques commonly used in the production of visual text. Below is an exercise to help you begin the process. Link the term with the correct definition in the grid below.

Terms

a		Colour
b		Alliteration
c		Font (style and size)
d		Layout
e		DVF
f		Graphic/illustration
g		Symbols/logos
h		Background
i		Empty space
j		Well-known/popular faces
k		Body copy
l		Repetition
m		Use of adjectives
n		Personal pronouns
o		Slogan
p		Rhetorical question

Definitions

1 Where a concrete object is used to represent one or more abstract ideas.

2 The dominant colour used as the base of the image. It may be left plain in order to focus the viewer's attention on the other features or it may incorporate colour to support its message.

3 The pictures, photographs, drawings, graphs – everything that is not just the writing in an image.

4 Can be used to help represent their product or idea. It can also be eye-catching.

5 The use of words such as 'you', 'we', 'our' to give a chatty, conversational tone to the piece to make the audience feel included.

6 Carefully chosen describing words that help us picture the look, taste or texture of the product.

7 The use of someone who is famous to sell a product/service. It may be purely to attract our attention or to endorse a product.

8 The repetition of the product name, slogan and/or key features to help ingrain the brand in your mind.

9 The detailed words in a visual text.

10 The central focus (point of impact) of the visual text.

11 Will reflect the ideas within the image. Must also be easy to read.

12 A short, snappy sentence that sums up a product or service. It is usually easy to remember.

13 Used to allow the audience to focus on and consider the posed question.

14 Used most commonly because it is easy to remember. It makes words flow together more easily and highlights key words and ideas.

15 The process of organising the forms, shapes, colours and any words into a balanced design. These choices are made with the purpose, topic and audience in mind.

16 Where nothing is printed. It is critical in helping highlight graphics and illustrations.

43

ISBN 9780170195935

Focus 1: Visual close reading

A comic strip is a series of cartoon drawings narrating an incident. They are usually humorous and appear first in magazines or newspapers. They have conventions, for example in the way speech and thoughts are shown, in the way loud sounds or movement are indicated. You can see all of these in the *Footrot Flats* example here.

1   What evidence is there that this is a cartoon set on a farm?

   _____

2   In which frame does Dog shout the loudest?

   _____

3   How does Murray Ball show that the fox terrier is still a puppy?

   _____

4   Find an example of colloquial (informal) language.

   _____

5   What does the cartoonist do to make sure that we know that Dog is thinking all this rather than talking like the boy, Rangi, does?

   _____

   _____

6   How does Dog work out what a fox terrier does? Explain this in your own words.

   _____

   _____

7   Murray Ball makes use of a play on words in this cartoon. What are the two words?
    Explain Dog's misunderstanding.

   _____

   _____

ISBN 9780170195935

8   Based on what you have read in the cartoon, what kind of a relationship does Rangi have with Wal?

_____

_____

9   What does the comic strip show us about Dog's character?

_____

_____

_____

Focus 2: Recap parts of speech

Read the following extract and find ONE example of the language features listed below.

> This piano rocks. It's better than the one at home and infinitely better than Todd's one – I don't know why they keep a piano in a garage anyway. I play and play and I can feel the stress slip out of my feet and my fingers, the music taking it and chucking it away.
>
> I pull out the manuscript and start on the music we've worked through again and again. I close my eyes and can hear Todd count us in Two, Three, Four then Michael and Chris starting in with drums and acoustic, one, two, three, four, I'm counting, hearing them and waiting for the eighth bar for me and Todd, one, two, three, four, then it's my turn. Da Da break. Da … Da, Da Da! Then, I'm away, into the melody, the one we wrote together and I can hear him singing.
>
> Playing and playing and playing right to the end. Michael's down beat once with Chris pushing through that last chord change and me waiting, hearing them, waiting till it's my turn to do the solo with just me and Todd … right to the end, light, sweeter, gentle, gentle, slower and then just me finishing, bringing it to closure.
>
> Perfect.
>
> From G-Force, Tania Roxborogh

Parts of speech

Nouns

– Concrete _____

– Proper _____

– Abstract _____

Personal pronoun _____

Adjective _____

Verb _____

Apostrophe for contraction _____

Apostrophe for possession _____

Look at chapter 2 of *How to …* to remind yourself of this.

Figurative language

Alliteration _____

Personification _____

Repetition _____

Types of language

Colloquial language _____

Jargon _____

Sentences

Simple sentence _____

Compound sentence _____

Minor sentence _____

A sentence written to suggest speed _____

A sentence written to suggest slowness _____

45

ISBN 9780170195935

Week _____ Date for completion _____

Parent's sig. _____ Teacher's sig. _____

Focus 1: Character essay

This activity asks you to write a clear, detailed, thoughtful essay. Complete the information in the box below before you begin.

Title of text: _____ Author of text: _____

Let's recap how to write a literary essay

By now you will be aware of the basic structure you can use to write your essay.

> ### Introduction
> This paragraph should always:
> - give the title and author (director, poet) of the text
> - give the genre (novel, short story, poem, film)
> - refer to the question.
>
> ### Body paragraphs
> The body of the essay is divided into paragraphs. How many will depend on the type of question you're asked. Generally a body paragraph should have:
> - a topic sentence that clearly states what the paragraph will be about
> - detail from the text
> - relevant quotations
> - explanation
> - a sentence to link back to the original idea.
>
> ### Conclusion
> This will include:
> - no new information (it shows a lack of prior planning)
> - a restatement of the main point of your essay, strongly referring back to the question.

Don't forget to use quotations to support your ideas. Go to page 98 of your *How to …* textbook to remind yourself on how to best incorporate quotations in your essay.

Let's have a look at the essay topic you have been given.

> **Describe an idea that interested you in the text. Explain why it interested you.**

Using a red or blue pen, annotate the question with the following:

- Put brackets around each part of the question.
- Underline the key words in the question.

In the box below decide upon the following things:

- List two possible relationships you could use for this topic. Think about main character(s) and their relationship with each other and with minor characters.
- For each relationship, brainstorm at least two reasons why this relationship was important to the text.
- Think about some of the following things: Did the relationship change? Did the relationship offer support to one character or both characters? Did it illustrate the idea/purpose/theme? Did the relationship create conflict/humour? Did the relationship reveal a character's personality or values?

ISBN 9780170195935

Evaluate the information you have in the box above. One relationship should stand out as being easier to write about than the others.
- Look through your handouts, character notes, and so on.
- Go back to the key places in the text and reread them. Take notes and copy suitable quotations.
- Use a different-colour pen to group and structure your information.

You should now be ready to begin writing your essay. Write the final copy of your essay in the back of this book.

Focus 2: Verbs and adverbs

Verbs

You will all know that a verb is a 'doing' or a 'being' word. Verbs are really very important because they can tell us so much. Imagine you are watching someone walk down the street. This person's way of *walking* can say so much. Is he:

ambling?	Suggests carefree, not in a hurry, no particular purpose.
hurrying?	Suggests late for something, worried, panicked.
skipping?	Suggests happy, lively, young, enjoyment.
limping?	Suggests injury, pain, discomfort, age.
shambling?	Suggests a tramp, a lack of motor control, a lack of purpose.

> When you're searching for a good word, a thesaurus is a marvellous help.

You do:

What do these verbs suggest to you? (Set out as above.)

crawled _____

dashed _____

hiked _____

marched _____

sauntered _____

stormed _____

trudged _____

waddled _____

sailed _____

Now try finding some alternatives to the well-used word *said*. Include what you want the word to suggest.

1 _____   _____

2 _____   _____

3 _____   _____

4 _____   _____

5 _____   _____

Adverbs

A great verb is better than a whole list of adverbs, but adverbs do have their uses. They describe verbs and they tell us when, where and how things happen. We will look just at adverbs of manner here – adverbs that say how something is being done. These adverbs often end in 'ly' (though not always).
For example:

Tomorrow I will walk **calmly** into the office and **politely** ask for my iPod back.

You do:

Replace the two adverbs of manner with others that change the tone of the sentence:

Tomorrow I will walk _____ into the office and _____ ask for my iPod back.

Tomorrow I will walk _____ into the office and _____ ask for my iPod back.

ISBN 9780170195935

Week _____ Date for completion _____

Parent's sig. _____ Teacher's sig. _____

Focus 1: Speech planning

Use the following activity to help formulate the ideas and structure of your speech.

Your topic is: _____

Remember to structure your speech

Opening
- Gets the audience's attention.
- Tells the audience what the topic is.
- Tells the audience what points to listen for. They are

_____

_____

_____

Your first point is

_____

_____

_____

- Backed up with what type of evidence?

_____

- Bridges the points with links to the next idea.

_____

_____

Your second point is

_____

_____

_____

- Backed up with what type of evidence?

_____

- Bridges the points with links to the next idea.

_____

_____

Your third point is

_____

_____

_____

- Backed up with what type of evidence?

_____

- Bridges the points with links to ideas.

_____

_____

Conclusion
- Summarises the presentation.
- Emphasises what you want the audience to remember, which is:

_____

You need to open your speech effectively. It is important that your audience wants to continue listening to your speech. Try to think of one each of the following for your topic.
- Shock them with a statistic/fact _____
- Ask a question _____
- Use a quotation _____
- Use a catchphrase_____
- Tell a story _____
- Create a link _____

You must back up your points with evidence. Try and incorporate a different method for each point you make. Try and think of one of each of the following for your topic.
- Statistics _____
- Historical facts _____
- A story (anecdote) _____
- Current event _____

You might like to incorporate some of the following into the body of your speech to make it more interesting. Write some sentences about your topic that use the features below.
- Alliteration _____
- Similes _____
- Rhyme _____
- Pun _____
- Catchphrases _____
- Onomatopoeia _____
- Metaphors _____

You need to ensure your audience remembers your speech. Try and include something that will hold in their mind after you have finished speaking. Try to think of one each of the following for your topic.
- Remind them of a shocking statistic _____
- Ask a rhetorical question _____
- Use a quote _____
- Use a catchphrase _____

You might like to use a visual aid to help keep your audience interested/involved. Think about how each of the following would be used in your speech.
- PowerPoint _____
- OHT/whiteboard _____
- Map _____
- Poster _____
- Having a handout _____

Show this information to your teacher before you go any further with your speech.

ISBN 9780170195935

Focus 2: Speechwriting techniques

You will have been asked by your teacher to include some language techniques while writing your speech, techniques that help to make your speech interesting for your audience. You could choose from any of the following:

| Personal pronouns | Emotive words | Listing | Colloquial language | Quotations | Anecdotes |
| Examples/statistics | Figures of speech | Repetition | Rhetorical questions | Humour | |

Let's take a look at a couple you might find useful – even if you think you know about them already.

Rhetorical question

A rhetorical question is a question put not to elicit an answer but to heighten the persuasive power of the writer or speaker. Often a speaker adds emphasis to a point by putting it in the form of a question, the answer to which supports his or her argument.

Speakers often use a rhetorical question at the beginning or end of their speech. At the beginning of the speech you can ask a question that will capture your audience's attention and get them involved in your speech and thinking about how it is relevant to them.

For example: *How many of you suffer from 'Bad Hair Days'?* (pause) *I can see many of you nodding your head …*

By using a rhetorical question at the end of your speech you will leave your audience something to think about. It may provoke them to make a change in their lives or to consider the issue beyond the end of your speech.

For example: *So, what will you do with your empty bottle next time you are faced with the dilemma of there being no bin in sight?*

Listing

Some speechwriters like to use the technique of listing. This is where they will 'list' several examples at once.

For example: *Whether it is you or I, Bono or Bob Geldof, Kofi Annan or Tony Blair, Angelina Jolie or the various statesmen for the African nations at the centre of this issue, it is firmly believed by a majority of people that something must be done about the crisis facing Africa today.*

The idea behind listing is that by providing your audience with lots of examples you are adding weight to your argument. In the above example the speech writer wanted to show that people from all walks of life, status and importance agree with the issue – emphasising that is not something trivial.

But be careful not to overuse this technique (any technique) or your speech will sound repetitive and you will risk losing the attention of your audience.

You do:

Use the following information to help you write a short (100-word) section of a speech on the topic 'The Importance of Recycling' that contains a rhetorical question and an example of listing.

Recycling is a process of making waste into new and different products.

Glass can become many things once recycled, so can paper.

Many people recycle plastic bottles and aluminium cans.

When shopping, remember to buy products that are recyclable or have recyclable packaging.

Avoid landfills.

Industry is good at recycling steel.

Kerbside collections.

The North Shore City Council collects about 16,339 tonnes of recyclables per year.

Reduce it. Reuse it. Recycle!

It will help to reduce future disposal costs.

Inorganic collections.

_____

_____

_____

_____

_____

_____

ISBN 9780170195935

Focus 1: Visual close reading

Whatever spins your wheels

...or floats your boat!

With so many quick and easy ways to prepare lean beef and lamb, you can choose exactly what you feel like and feel twice as good!

BEEF + LAMB
Feel Twice as Good
www.recipes.co.nz

ISBN 9780170195935

Read the advertisement through carefully and highlight/annotate the **layout** elements of a visual text. Then look for as many examples of **verbal techniques** and **visual techniques** as you can possibly find. Make sure you do this tidily. Do not ruin your ability to see the overall image.

Layout
- Headline
- Image
- Body copy
- Background
- Logo/slogan

Verbal techniques
Pronouns
Alliteration
Rhyme
Adjectives
Repetition
Slogan
Pun/play on words

Visual techniques
Empty space
Headline
DVF
Use of celebrity
Symbol

Now you have spent some time analysing the advertisement, answer the questions that follow.

1 Explain the connection between the headline 'Whatever spins your wheels … or floats your boat' to the rest of the image.

_____
_____
_____
_____

2 Explain the connection of the repeated phrase 'feel twice as good' to the rest of the image.

_____
_____
_____
_____

3 Explain the connection of the phrase 'so many quick and easy ways to prepare lean beef and lamb' to the rest of the image.

_____
_____
_____
_____

Focus 2: Punctuation practice

Read the passage and then answer the questions that follow.

^{1}**F**or nearly fifty years, Scott Base has been New Zealand's^2 base in Antarctica. It houses about eighty people over the summer,^{3} although only about ten or twelve of them stay for the long dark winter. Many of them are scientists, but there are also support staff, who all have important jobs ^{4}– people like chefs,^{5} kitchen hands, cleaners, mechanics and engineers.

In Antarctica, you use up lots of energy just keeping warm, so you need good, nutritious food to keep up your energy levels. But if you're living at ^{6}**S**cott **B**ase, you can't duck out to the local takeaways for a snack – and the chefs can^7't just pop out to the supermarket, either. In fact, feeding the community at Scott Base takes a lot of organisation because everything has to come in from outside Antarctica. Every aspect,^{8} from ordering the food to storing it and disposing of the leftovers, has to be carefully thought out.

Explain why each numbered punctuation mark has been used:

1 _____
2 _____
3 _____
4 _____
5 _____
6 _____
7 _____
8 _____

ISBN 9780170195935

Focus 1: Sentences make sense

Read this passage:

> It is one thousand years ago a moa walks out of a South Island forest and into scrubland it is very wary looking repeatedly at the sky it begins feeding on smaller plants pruning them like hedge clippers This moa is the biggest flightless bird in the world it weighs almost 200 kilograms nearly twice the weight of Jonah Lomu for the moment, it thinks it's safe it isn't

Not that easy, is it? If you read it aloud you will naturally put in pauses to make it make sense.

When people talk to you, they put in pauses to make what they are saying easy to understand. It's the same with writing: the punctuation is there to help the reader get to the meaning of the words easily as he or she reads. Help your reader by using punctuation to create sense. Writing, whether in school, at your place of work or in an email to a friend, that is not punctuated properly shows your teacher, employer, correspondent that you are not able to express yourself adequately or you don't care enough to write properly.

You do:

Rewrite the passage above using full stops, commas and capital letters to make it easier to understand.

_____
_____
_____
_____
_____
_____
_____

At this stage we would like you to think about using different sentence shapes:

1 The short, simple sentence with just one idea.
   For example: The owl and the pussycat went to sea.
2 The compound sentence with two or more ideas joined together.
   For example: The owl looked up at the stars above and sang to a small guitar.
3 The longer sentence with more details (we won't go into the grammar here but if you want to, look up compound-complex sentences on the Internet).
   For example: They took some honey and plenty of money, tied up in a five-pound note.

You do:

Write a short (six sentences at the most) passage that describes a recent journey you have made. Try to use these three sorts of sentences.

_____
_____
_____
_____
_____
_____

If you know you have trouble with sentences, here's another passage where the full stops and capital letters are missing. Read the passage aloud to see what it means and then put in the punctuation.

> horses are wonderful they're so beautiful but I can't have one, even though I really, really want one I don't even ask it costs a lot of money to buy a horse and then more to feed it and to pay to use a paddock we don't have that kind of money
>
> what I do instead is I draw horses I love to draw them I have a special artist's block with stiff, thick, white paper in it my mum gave it to me for my birthday I draw my best pictures in there I take a lot of time and use only pencil, and I rub out really carefully so I don't make a mess

Try and be vigilant with your full stops this week.

ISBN 9780170195935

Let's stop and take another look at the 'little' words that help hold a sentence together.

Prepositions

A preposition's job in a sentence is to join nouns or pronouns to other words in a sentence. Prepositions show relationships (for example the place, direction or distance) between one thing or person and another. One good way to remember this is prepositions show position.

Examples of prepositions are:

in	out	under	over	beside	between	towards	across
about	inside	without	through	beneath	into	up	down

You do:

Write the directions for getting from your house to the nearest beach (or supermarket, if you don't live next to the beach). Use at least five prepositions like 'down', 'across', 'under', 'beside' and 'over'.

_____

_____

_____

_____

Conjunctions

Essentially a conjunction glues parts of a sentence together. Conjunctions are connecting words that join two or more sentences into a single sentence. They can also join words, phrases or clauses.

Joining two words: **The day was sunny and windy.**

Joining two sentences to make one sentence: **It was perfect for sailing so we headed for the marina.**

Conjunctions are usually found in the middle of sentences, but some may be used to begin a sentence.

The boat sailed beautifully well although it was small.

could be written as:

Although the boat was small, it sailed beautifully well.

Choosing the correct conjunction depends on what you want to say. Look at these examples:

Jean likes toast and cereal for breakfast.
Jean likes toast but prefers cereal for breakfast.
Jean likes toast or cereal for breakfast.

Each sentence says something different because of the conjunction that has been chosen.

You do:

Examples of conjunctions are as follows.

Relating to time:	since, before, after, until, till, as soon as, while, when, yet
Relating to contrast:	however, while, whereas, although
Relating to result:	so, so that, such, that
Relating to comparison:	as, than, like, as if, though
Relating to cause:	as, because, for

Write five sentences using one conjunction from each of the lists above.

1 _____

2 _____

3 _____

4 _____

5 _____

ISBN 9780170195935

Week _____ Date for completion _____

Parent's sig. _____ Teacher's sig. _____

Focus 1: Understanding poetry

Have go at translating this poem in the space provided on the right-hand side of the page.

Fone Filosfy

luv
is a nrvus rng
Ch@rin thru yr ♥
wearing valvt sliprs
n a roz bhin hr ear
hidin a chocl8 bx bhin hr bak

shock
a sombr call
stmpin n da door
@ 2 in da morn
wakin da dog n naybrs
leavn a blak egd telgrm
n da dorstp

xitmnt
s a rng
dat swoops n swrls
n rozy culrs roun ur cheeks
btrflyn tru ur tum

n life
is axeptin dat sumtims
silnce
cn say mor dn ny telfon
dat rngs 4 u

by Louise Phyn

Phone Philosophy

_____

_____

_____

_____

_____

_____

_____

_____

_____

_____

_____

_____

_____

_____

_____

_____

_____

_____

_____

_____

_____

_____

_____

The first three stanzas each talk about a different way that cellphones are used today to communicate so many significant events. The message of the poem is found in the last stanza. In your own words explain what you think the poet is saying.

_____

_____

_____

_____

_____

ISBN 9780170195935

Focus 2a: New languages – texting and emailing

Recent developments in technology such as email and cellphones have created a new language. The language of text and email is informal and generally does not adhere to grammatical rules.

You will find you use acronyms:

FAQ	Frequently Asked Questions	lol	laugh out loud
rofl	roll on floor laughing	DW	don't worry
TB	text back	ty	thank you
brb	be right back	btw	by the way
cu	see you		

You might even use emoticons:

:-)	happy/smiling	:-))	very happy
:-(	sad	:-o	surprised/shocked
:-O	bored	%-)	confused
:')	crying	;-P	Tongue in cheek

Be careful – it may be appropriate for you to use this style of language when texting or emailing but it is not appropriate for formal writing in essays, letters, and so on.

You do:

Have a go at either:

Writing a series of text messages that use e-language.

Or   Translating a piece of writing into e-language. (Don't forget to attach a copy of the original piece of writing.)

Or   Writing your own poem using e-language.

_____

_____

_____

_____

_____

_____

_____

_____

_____

Focus 2b: Formal writing

Do you have a cellphone? Do you send and receive text messages? You probably answered 'yes' to both of these questions. There is a lot of debate about whether cellphones cause more problems than they create. Most teenagers in New Zealand have a phone and are very familiar with text. However, when the abbreviated language of the text message jumps into email, appears in books, has scholarly articles written about it and starts to be used in teenagers' schoolwork and school rooms, then it's time to stop and think. Is this a good thing or a bad thing? What is your opinion?

You do:

Choose one of the following topics and write an essay to persuade your teacher that you are right.

Teenagers need cellphones.
Text-messaging serves an important purpose.
A teenager needs a cellphone like a fish needs a bicycle.
Cellphones ruin family life.
Text is just as good for communication as ordinary writing.
Teenagers don't talk any more; they text instead.
Text language has its place in today's world.
Why teenagers use text messaging.

You will already have written several formal essays this year. Either turn to page 30 of this book or chapter 6 in *How to …* for a quick recap of the process and structure of a formal essay.

Write the final copy of your piece in the back of this book.

ISBN 9780170195935

Week _____ Date for completion _____

Parent's sig. _____ Teacher's sig. _____

Focus 1: Speech marks

Inverted commas

You know what these are but you may be more familiar with the name 'speech marks' or 'quotation marks'. These names come from what we use them for: to show in writing what is a quotation or what is direct speech.

The name inverted commas is because they are made of commas; the first one or set is up (") and the second is inverted, turned upside down (").

You may use either one inverted comma or two. Just be sure that they match. If you use two at the beginning of a quotation you must use two at the end. So "…" or '…' – it's up to you.	If you want to put a quotation within a quotation use single marks inside double marks. For example, "When I say 'now' I mean right this minute!" said Dad.

Using inverted commas in dialogue

Put the words actually spoken inside the speech marks. All other words are outside. For example:

'You boys all set for tomorrow?' asked Ms Lyons, our music teacher.
Abe gave one of his huge grins. 'Man, we are the best!' he said. Tere and Reuben laughed and agreed. I smiled, too, but only on the outside.

Remember that all the punctuation belonging to the spoken words goes inside the speech marks. That's a little detail that trips students up – you read it here! Also remember that:

- the first word inside the inverted commas begins with a capital letter if it's the start of the speaker's words. If the spoken sentence is broken, then the second part will not use a capital letter. Here's an example:
  'We're going to play brilliantly,' smiled Tere, *'and win!'*
- you use a new paragraph for each new speaker.

Direct or reported?

Direct speech is where the exact words of the speaker are used. For instance: Mum asked, 'Where is the remote control?'

Reported speech is where what has been said is 'reported' back. For instance: Mum asked where the remote control was.

When you are writing your own stories it is good to incorporate a mixture of direct and reported speech. Variety in all things keeps your writing fresh.

You do:

Correctly punctuate the following passage. You will need to use capital letters, full stops, commas, apostrophes, inverted commas and an exclamation mark!

no way mum im not going vicky glared at the rusty van juddering down the farm road towards them there are heaps of kids in the back please dont make me get in with them

why not asked mum you might enjoy it id say theyre off to kill the pig for the birthday

ugh thats disgusting you want your only daughter to witness the killing of an innocent animal

the driver of the van must have noticed mums silver four-wheel-drive he waved and tooted and swung the wheel towards the gate

mum …vicky pleaded

it'll give you a chance to get to know some of the kids from the marae

ISBN 9780170195935

Focus 2: Proofreading

Use a capital letter for:
- the start of every new sentence
- using the word 'I'
- days of the week
- months of the year
- names of people, places
- important words in the title of books, television programmes and films.

Use a full stop at:
- the end of every sentence.

Use a comma to:
- divide a sentence into parts, making the ideas easier to identify
- separate items in a list.

Use an apostrophe to:
- show ownership
- show where letters are missed out in a contraction.

You do:

1 Correct the following paragraph, putting in the correct punctuation. It might be a good idea to start in pencil.

campbell island is the southernmost island of new zealand it lies on the 52nd parallel southeast of the auckland islands 600 kilometres from stewart island it is the remains of an extinct volcano its highest peak rises 550 metres above the southern ocean its western sides are steep with rocky ledges and sheer cliffs there are few sheltered coves and sandy bays the island slopes towards the east which is more sheltered from the strong westerly and antarctic winds in the frequent gales wind speed is around 34 knots (about 55 km per hour) gusting up to 70–80 knots (110–130 km per hour) with rain hail and sleet in a hurricane, gusts can rise to 240 km per hour it is often cold but even in the winter the snow doesnt stay around for long because the sea temperature of 7 or 8 degrees Celsius keeps the land warm the average annual temperature is 6 degrees and in the brief summer doesn't go much above 12 but the sky is light then until eleven at night

Just to be nice we thought we'd let you know that the author of this extract included:

| 20 capital letters | 12 full stops | 10 commas | 1 apostrophe |

2 Read the sentences below carefully. Then complete the chart below by writing which part of speech each word belongs to. We have already done a few to get you started.

As	the	young	man	reached	the	top	of
						Noun	

the	ridge	a	black	helicopter	suddenly	clattered	noisily

into	view.	He	lifted	his	hands	to	his
				Poss. pronoun			

ears,	protecting	them	from	its	noisy	din.	
	Verb						

Punctuation fascinates some people. If you're such a person, try looking on the Internet for all the very specific rules that exist regarding the use of punctuation – this is just the tip of the iceberg.

ISBN 9780170195935

Week _____ Date for completion _____

Parent's sig. _____ Teacher's sig. _____

Focus 1: Who makes movies?

Use either the library or the Internet to help you complete the following exercise.

1 Describe what each of the following phases of film making are. Give some examples of tasks likely to be completed in each.

Pre-production _____

_____

Production _____

_____

Post-production _____

_____

2 What role does each of the following play in the pre-production, production or post-production of a film?

Producer _____

Director _____

Production assistant _____

Director of photography/cinematography _____

Grip _____

Scriptwriter _____

Editor _____

Continuity _____

Costume designer _____

Foley editor _____

Composer _____

Gaffer _____

Location manager _____

3 Find three other roles *not* mentioned in Question 2 and explain what each job entails.

1 _____

2 _____

3 _____

ISBN 9780170195935

Focus 2: Pronouns

You all know that a pronoun takes the place of a noun. Let's take some time to recap pronouns.

Sort the pronouns

Sort the pronouns below into 'possessive' and 'personal' by putting them into the table.

| mine | I | yours | she | ours | you | me | |
| he | its | it | hers | her | his | him | theirs |

Personal pronouns (describe a person or thing)	Possessive pronouns (describe who or what belongs)

Find the pronouns

Highlight all the pronouns. If you can, use two colours to show personal and possessive pronouns.

1. He went outside to find them.
2. We asked her if she was feeling all right.
3. Do you know if they want to come with us?
4. It isn't yours; it's mine!
5. They took me home in their car.
6. I will have dinner when they come home.
7. We didn't know if she was in our team.
8. He plays cricket for them every week.

Use a pronoun

Fill in the gaps from the sentences below using pronouns instead of the bracketed nouns.

	Singular pronouns	Plural pronouns
When the pronoun is the subject of the sentence.	I you he she it	We You they
When the pronoun is the object in a sentence.	me you him her it	us you them
When the pronoun shows that something belongs to someone.	mine yours his hers its	our(s) your(s) their(s)

1. **(Riley and Mia)** _____ hid in the garden from **(Dad)** _____.

2. **(Jodie)** _____ wrote a letter on **(Jodie's)** _____ computer.

3. **(Greer)** _____ stroked the cat and listened to **(the cat)** _____ purring happily.

4. **(Riley)** _____ went into the TV room to find **(Riley's)** _____ sisters.

5. **'(The trophy)** is **(the team's trophy)!'** _____ the team exclaimed.

Why a pronoun?

Ask yourself: *why* is a pronoun used? In the most straightforward situation a pronoun is to ensure that we are not irritated with having the same name repeated over and over again in a text, a conversation, a film: anywhere, in fact. Here's the start of a children's story:

> Riley and Mia wanted to go into the garden and jump on the trampoline. Riley and Mia asked Mum if Riley and Mia could go outside. The only problem was Riley and Mia's mum had banned Riley and Mia from the tramp after Riley and Mia had spent all morning fighting over the smallest things. Riley had an idea. Riley whispered Riley's plan into Mia's ear. Mia nodded, and Riley and Mia crept under Riley and Mia's beds and tried to keep silent, waiting for Mum to start looking for Riley and Mia.

Put the pronouns 'he', 'she', 'they', 'their', 'he', 'she', 'them' in the spaces left for them and you will make the passage sound less repetitive.

> Riley and Mia wanted to go into the garden and jump on the trampoline. _____ asked Mum if _____ could go outside. The only problem was _____ mum had banned _____ from the tramp after _____ had spent all morning fighting over the smallest things. Riley had an idea. _____ whispered _____ plan into Mia's ear. _____ nodded, and _____ crept under _____ beds and tried to keep silent, waiting for Mum to start looking for _____.

Being able to use pronouns effectively will help you to improve your own writing.

59

Week _____ Date for completion _____

Parent's sig. _____ Teacher's sig. _____

Focus 1: Visual close reading

E kuri: Hey dog   Hikina te wero: Take up the challenge   Kokopu: native fish

Read the advertisement through carefully and highlight/annotate the **layout** elements of a visual text.

Then look for as many examples of **verbal techniques** and **visual techniques** as you can possibly find. Make sure you do this tidily. Do not ruin your ability to see the overall image.

Layout	Visual techniques	Verbal techniques	
• Headline	Point of contrast	Proper noun	Use of adjectives for effect
• Image	Bold lettering	Colloquial language	Personal pronouns
• Body copy	Logos	Cliché	Alliteration
• Background	Balance	Tone of language	Contraction
• Logo/slogan	Reverse type	Repetition	Maori (local flavour)
	Conventions of cartoons		

Now you have spent some time analysing the advertisement, answer the questions that follow.

1 There are two things being advertised in this advertisement. What are they?

_____

_____

2 What is the connection between the two parts of the advertisement?

_____

_____

3 How have they made the two sections of the advertisement different from each other?

_____

_____

ISBN 9780170195935

4 How are the two parts of the advertisement joined together? _____

_____

5 How many logos appear on the advertisement? _____

6 How many ways can you find out more about what is being talked about in the advertisement?

_____

7 Can you see a difference in the language between the left and right of the advertisement? Explain?

_____

_____

8 Who do you think the target audience is and why? _____

_____

9 Why is the word 'sewerage' put in brackets? _____

10 Look carefully at the headline for the right-hand side of the advertisement. Why is the word 'dog' in bold?

_____

_____

11 How does the sign in frame 6 back up the overall message? _____

_____

Focus 2: Word origin

Where do our words come from?

English is a language that has 'borrowed' words from many other languages (with no intention of giving them back). One of the significant sources is Greek. Indeed, the word 'alphabet' is from the two words 'alpha' (A) and 'beta' (B), which are the first two letters of the Greek alphabet.

Lots of words in English are spelt using 'ph' to make the sound 'f', words like pharmacy, phase and phenomenon; geography, graph and hyphen.

Can you find the words to fit these meanings? They all have 'ph' making the sound 'f' in them and they are all of Greek origin.

1 Huge four-footed pachyderm

_____

2 Child with deceased parents

_____

3 Apparatus for transmitting speech

_____

4 Picture taken by means of chemical action of light on sensitive film

_____

5 Science dealing with matter and energy

_____

6 Ancient Egyptian kings

_____

Getting trickier:

7 The study of clouds

_____

8 Practical benevolence towards mankind

_____

9 Lover of wisdom

_____

10 Change of form by magic or natural development

Another major source of words in English is French. French-speaking people were in charge in England for about 300 years, starting in 1066. Many words entered English from French at this time and lots of them are connected with the law, government and the ruling classes. Use an etymological dictionary to find these words, and where they are from:

1 tax _____

2 parliament _____

3 countess _____

4 legal _____

5 jury _____

6 court _____

7 duke _____

8 aristocrat _____

9 government _____

10 regal _____

ISBN 9780170195935

Focus: Putting it all together

All Summer in a Day

Ray Bradbury

'Ready?'

'Ready.'

'Now?'

'Soon.'

'Do the scientists really know? Will it happen today, will it?'

'Look, look; see for yourself!'

The children pressed to each other like so many roses, so many weeds, intermixed, peering out for a look at the hidden sun.

It rained.

It had been raining for seven years; thousands upon thousands of days compounded and filled from one end to the other with rain, with the drum and gush of water, with the sweet crystal fall of showers and the concussion of storms so heavy they were tidal waves come over the islands. A thousand forests had been crushed under the rain and grown up a thousand times to be crushed again. And this was the way life was forever on the planet Venus, and this was the schoolroom of the children of the rocket men and women who had come to a raining world to set up civilization and live out their lives.

'It's stopping, it's stopping!'

'Yes, yes!'

Margot stood apart from them, from these children who could never remember a time when there wasn't rain and rain and rain. They were all nine years old, and if there had been a day, seven years ago, when the sun came out for an hour and showed its face to the stunned world, they could not recall. Sometimes, at night, she heard them stir, in remembrance, and she knew they were dreaming and remembering gold or a yellow crayon or a coin large enough to buy the world with. She knew they thought they remembered a warmness, like a blushing in the face, in the body, in the arms and legs and trembling hands. But then they always awoke to the tatting drum, the endless shaking down of clear bead necklaces upon the roof, the walk, the gardens, the forests, and their dreams were gone.

All day yesterday they had read in class about the sun. About how like a lemon it was, and how hot. And they had written small stories or essays or poems about it:

I think the sun is a flower,
That blooms for just one hour.

That was Margot's poem, read in a quiet voice in the still classroom while the rain was falling outside.

'Aw, you didn't write that!' protested one of the boys.

'I did," said Margot. 'I did.'

'William!' said the teacher.

But that was yesterday. Now the rain was slackening, and the children were crushed in the great thick windows.

Where's teacher?'

'She'll be back.'

'She'd better hurry, we'll miss it!'

They turned on themselves, like a feverish wheel, all tumbling spokes. Margot stood alone. She was a very frail girl who looked as if she had been lost in the rain for years and the rain had washed out the blue from her eyes and the red from her mouth and the yellow from her hair. She was an old photograph dusted from an album, whitened away, and if she spoke at all her voice would be a ghost. Now she stood, separate, staring at the rain and the loud wet world beyond the huge glass.

'What're *you* looking at?' said William.

Margot said nothing.

'Speak when you're spoken to.'

He gave her a shove. But she did not move; rather she let herself be moved only by him and nothing else. They edged away from her, they would not look at her. She felt them go away. And this was because she would play no games with them in the echoing tunnels of the underground city. If they tagged her and ran, she stood blinking after them and did not follow. When the class sang songs about happiness and life and games her lips barely moved. Only when they sang about the sun and the summer did her lips move as she watched the drenched windows. And then, of course, the biggest crime of all was that she had come here only five years ago from Earth, and she remembered the sun and the way the sun was and the sky was when she was four in Ohio. And they, they had been on Venus all their lives, and they had been only two years old when last the sun came out and had long since forgotten the colour and heat of it and the way it really was.

But Margot remembered.

'It's like a penny,' she said once, eyes closed.

'No it's not!' the children cried.

'It's like a fire,' she said, 'in the stove.'

'You're lying, you don't remember!' cried the children.

But she remembered and stood quietly apart from all of them and watched the patterning windows. And once, a month ago, she had refused to shower in the school shower rooms, had clutched her hands to her ears and over her head, screaming the water mustn't touch her head. So after that, dimly, dimly, she sensed it, she was different and they knew her difference and kept away. There was talk that her father and mother were taking

ISBN 9780170195935

her back to Earth next year; it seemed vital to her that they do so, though it would mean the loss of thousands of dollars to her family. And so, the children hated her for all these reasons of big and little consequence. They hated her pale snow face, her waiting silence, her thinness, and her possible future.

'Get away!' The boy gave her another push. 'What're you waiting for?'

Then, for the first time, she turned and looked at him. And what she was waiting for was in her eyes.

'Well, don't wait around here!' cried the boy savagely. 'You won't see nothing!'

Her lips moved.

'Nothing!' he cried. 'It was all a joke, wasn't it?' He turned to the other children. 'Nothing's happening today. *Is* it?'

They all blinked at him and then, understanding, laughed and shook their heads.

'Nothing, nothing!'

'Oh, but,' Margot whispered, her eyes helpless. 'But this is the day, the scientists predict, they say, they *know*, the sun …'

'All a joke!' said the boy, and seized her roughly. 'Hey, everyone, let's put her in a closet before the teacher comes!'

'No,' said Margot, falling back.

They surged about her, caught her up and bore her, protesting, and then pleading, and then crying, back into a tunnel, a room, a closet, where they slammed and locked the door. They stood looking at the door and saw it tremble from her beating and throwing herself against it. They heard her muffled cries. Then, smiling, they turned and went out and back down the tunnel, just as the teacher arrived.

'Ready, children?' She glanced at her watch.

'Yes!' said everyone.

'Are we all here?'

'Yes!'

The rain slacked still more.

They crowded to the huge door.

The rain stopped.

It was as if, in the midst of a film concerning an avalanche, a tornado, a hurricane, a volcanic eruption, something had, first, gone wrong with the sound apparatus, thus muffling and finally cutting off all noise, all of the blasts and repercussions and thunders, and then, second, ripped the film from the projector and inserted in its place a beautiful tropical slide which did not move or tremor. The world ground to a standstill. The silence was so immense and unbelievable that you felt your ears had been stuffed or you had lost your hearing altogether. The children put their hands to their ears. They stood apart. The door slid back and the smell of the silent, waiting world came in to them.

The sun came out.

It was the colour of flaming bronze and it was very large. And the sky around it was a blazing blue tile colour. And the jungle burned with sunlight as the children, released from their spell, rushed out, yelling into the springtime.

'Now, don't go too far,' called the teacher after them.

'You've only two hours, you know. You wouldn't want to get caught out!'

But they were running and turning their faces up to the sky and feeling the sun on their cheeks like a warm iron; they were taking off their jackets and letting the sun burn their arms.

'Oh, it's better than the sun lamps, isn't it?'

'Much, much better!'

They stopped running and stood in the great jungle that covered Venus, that grew and never stopped growing, tumultuously, even as you watched it. It was a nest of octopi, clustering up great arms of fleshlike weed, wavering, flowering in this brief spring. It was the colour of rubber and ash, this jungle, from the many years without sun. It was the colour of stones and white cheeses and ink, and it was the colour of the moon.

The children lay out, laughing, on the jungle mattress, and heard it sigh and squeak under them resilient and alive. They ran among the trees, they slipped and fell, they pushed each other, they played hide-and-seek and tag, but most of all they squinted at the sun until the tears ran down their faces; they put their hands up to that yellowness and that amazing blueness and they breathed of the fresh, fresh air and listened and listened to the silence which suspended them in a blessed sea of no sound and no motion. They looked at everything and savoured everything. Then, wildly, like animals escaped from their caves, they ran and ran in shouting circles. They ran for an hour and did not stop running.

And then –

In the midst of their running one of the girls wailed.

Everyone stopped.

The girl, standing in the open, held out her hand.

'Oh, look, look,' she said, trembling.

They came slowly to look at her opened palm.

In the centre of it, cupped and huge, was a single raindrop. She began to cry, looking at it. They glanced quietly at the sun.

'Oh. Oh.'

A few cold drops fell on their noses and their cheeks and their mouths. The sun faded behind a stir of mist. A wind blew cold around them. They turned and started to walk back toward the underground house, their hands at their sides, their smiles vanishing away.

A boom of thunder startled them and like leaves before a new hurricane, they tumbled upon each other and ran. Lightning struck ten miles away, five miles away, a mile, a half mile. The sky darkened into midnight in a flash.

They stood in the doorway of the underground for a moment until it was raining hard. Then they closed the door and heard the gigantic sound of the rain falling in tons and avalanches, everywhere and forever.

'Will it be seven more years?'

'Yes. Seven.'

Then one of them gave a little cry.

'Margot!'

'What?'

'She's still in the closet where we locked her.'

'Margot.'

ISBN 9780170195935

They stood as if someone had driven them, like so many stakes, into the floor. They looked at each other and then looked away. They glanced out at the world that was raining now and raining and raining steadily. They could not meet each other's glances. Their faces were solemn and pale. They looked at their hands and feet, their faces down.

'Margot.'

One of the girls said, 'Well …?'

No one moved.

'Go on,' whispered the girl.

They walked slowly down the hall in the sound of cold rain. They turned through the doorway to the room in the sound of the storm and thunder, lightning on their faces, blue and terrible. They walked over to the closet door slowly and stood by it.

Behind the closet door was only silence.

They unlocked the door, even more slowly, and let Margot out.

Task 1: Understanding the story

1 What does this passage show about the change in the students' attitude?

'They stood as if someone had driven them with so many stakes into the floor. They looked at each other and then looked away … They could not meet each other's glances. Their faces were solemn and pale. They looked at their hands and feet, their faces down.'

a They now feel sorry for Margot.
b They are sad about the rain starting again so soon.
c They now realise how cruel they have been.
d All of the above.
e None of the above.

2 What does the title of the story mean?

a It all happened on a summer day.
b Since the period of sun was so short, the kids were forced to live a whole summer in a day.
c The summer seemed like it lasted only a day.
d The days are long in the summer.

3 What point is made about Margot when the story says that the rain had washed 'the blue from her eyes and the red from her mouth and the yellow from her hair'?

a The lack of sun is making her pale.
b She hated the rain.
c She was very sensitive to rain.
d The rain was draining the life out of her.

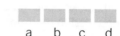

4 Locking Margot up is especially mean because …

a she is afraid of the dark.
b sunshine is so rare on this planet.
c she has no friends.
d she cries when she is locked up.

5 The main purpose of the story is probably …

a to provide a picture of what everyday life on Venus might be like.
b to show how weather conditions can affect your personality.
c to show how nine-year-old kids are.
d to show how differences can make some people a target for others.

6 Margot's background makes her feel …

a different from her classmates.
b better than her classmates.
c sympathetic toward her classmates because they haven't seen the sun.
d angry toward her classmates.

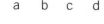

7 The *main* conflict of the story was …

a the kids of Venus vs. the rain and nature.
b William vs. Margot.
c The kids vs. someone different.
d Margot vs. the teacher for not helping her.
e the kids vs. themselves.

ISBN 9780170195935

8   The first thing the kids notice as soon as the rain stops is …
    a   the warmth.
    b   the brightness.
    c   the mud everywhere.
    d   the silence.

    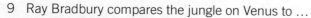

    a   b   c   d

9   Ray Bradbury compares the jungle on Venus to …
    a   tentacles of an octopus.
    b   the colour of white cheese.
    c   the colour of the moon.
    d   all of the above.
    e   none of the above.

    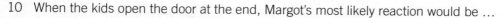

    a   b   c   d   e

10 When the kids open the door at the end, Margot's most likely reaction would be …
    a   to scream and attack William for making her miss the sun.
    b   to run outside into the rain.
    c   to sit in the corner of the closet crying.
    d   to yell at the teacher to punish William and the kids.

    a   b   c   d

Task 2: Character

Write a brief character study of Margot. Include the following:

- Her physical appearance
- Her personality
- Her relationship to others.

Use the pages at the back of this book to write your final copy.

Task 3: Theme

Write a 200–250 word essay which explores what this short story tells you about either:

> How individuality can lead to jealousy.
> OR
> How discrimination hurts people.

Try to apply the ideas in the story to your classroom world here on Earth.

Task 4: Creative writing

One of the effective techniques in *All Summer in a Day* is Ray Bradbury's ability to describe the setting of Venus before and while the sun comes out. To do this he uses many of the language techniques listed above. Your job is to write a passage in a similar descriptive style as 'All Summer in a Day'. You do not need to involve characters, just concentrate on setting. You can choose between:

- A grey world where for only one day every seven years colours appear.
- A very windy world where the wind stops for three hours every seven years.

You should attempt to involve as many language techniques as you can (without going overboard). You should aim to write about three-quarters of a page. You should start with a rough copy but make sure that you correct your punctuation and spelling once finished.

Delving deeper

In the film version of this story, the ending is handled differently. The children have come inside with huge bunches of flowers. When Margot is let out of the closet, she goes to one of the children and takes a flower and she walks across to William and gives it to him. Do you think Bradbury would have liked the different ending? Is his ending better? Why or why not? Write your answer into the back of the book.

ISBN 9780170195935

Focus: Putting it all together

Read the passage below and answer the questions that follow.

Winter and Summer in Bannockburn
Oliver Miller

On clear summer mornings in Bannockburn, the birds are so loud it sounds like a symphony orchestra. Frogs burp in the swamp at the base of the cliff in front of the lawn, and lizards, the length of pencils, bask on the pile of flat white stones by the hot tub. In the hazy distance, bald brown hills hunch like the bare bones of Gollum's back.

There is an old bathtub made of tin, which is always full of dirty rainwater and leaves, and it sits in the corner of the lawn. Tadpoles live in the bathtub, so sometimes, very early into the morning, a small neon-blue kingfisher comes and perches on the rim, dipping into the grubby water with his long, blade-shaped beak.

Beside the bathtub is a new, varnished, wooden hot tub, which is barely ever used in summer, so it sits there dormant like a volcano.

The wooden single-storied house has a large verandah, which is always full of odds and ends. An ancient out-of-tune piano, getting more so in the summer heat; a little tricycle covered in spider webs. There are beds with enormous mosquito nets hanging above them like ominous, grey rainclouds and boxes and boxes of tinned peaches lining the edge of the house.

When there has been a clear night, a heavy dew coats the grass, freezing desperate feet running for the out-house dunny. Later, on a hot day, a warm northerly wind starts to blow, and the tall poplars, on a ridge behind the house, shake and rustle their silvery leaves as if in jealousy of the sheltered, dusty pine down the drive.

Bannockburn is a place visited all year round. In winter the verandah is filled with boxes of driftwood and pinecones for the fire. Frost coats everything in the early morning and the birds are too cold to sing their songs. The old bathtub is frozen and the tadpoles are long gone, pursuing froggy futures in the swamp. Wet clothes left out on the lines are turned to cardboard.

In the morning the kitchen is a bustle of activity, full of people wrapped up in colourful skigear, warming toes by the fire or gobbling a breakfast of hot bacon and eggs at the table.

At night the dormant hot tub erupts into action, sending clouds of warm steam into the freezing air. When filled to the brim with hot, glittering water, it thaws out cold toes and hands from a day's skiing. The hot tub has been the site of many shivering and giggly grundy runs in wet togs. These are followed by a swift beating, with a rock-solid frozen t-shirt, of the people who laughed at the victim.

Late at night, when the hot tub is empty and the water gone cold, the house sheds deliciously golden light over the icy lawn and verandah. People sit around inside, sleepily basking in the warmth of the driftwood fire, playing cards or reading some of the vast collections of comics.

People always enjoy themselves at Bannockburn, no matter what the season.

1 Think carefully about what you have read and see if you can work out what you think the student writer's task was. Briefly explain.

_____

_____

_____

_____

_____

2 If you came up with something along the lines of describing a particular place that the student knows well, good job. Explain how you know that the student is very familiar with this house in Bannockburn.

_____

_____

_____

_____

ISBN 9780170195935

3   No doubt you have also picked up that the student has compared the house (and surrounding area) in summer to that of winter. Carefully read through the passage again. This time note in particular the things that have been compared in both parts. You may want to use a highlighter to make it easier.

4   When we read and compare the two parts of the passage we found five direct comparisons. Using what you found out in the previous question, complete the following grid. We've done the first one for you.

Bannockburn in summer	Bannockburn in winter
The birds are so loud it sounds like a symphony orchestra.	The birds are too cold to sing their song.

5   Now we've had a good look at what the student has done with the content of the piece, let's look at how he has used language to convey his environment so clearly. Let's have a look at the first paragraph together.

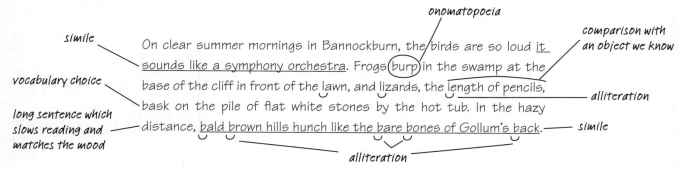

Now you have a go annotating this extract.

The wooden single-storied house has a large verandah, which is always full of odds and ends. An ancient out-of-tune piano, getting more so in the summer heat; a little tricycle covered in spider webs. There are beds with enormous mosquito nets hanging above them like ominous, grey rainclouds and boxes and boxes of tinned peaches lining the edge of the house.

When there has been a clear night, a heavy dew coats the grass, freezing desperate feet running for the out-house dunny. Later, on a hot day, a warm northerly wind starts to blow, and the tall poplars, on a ridge behind the house, shake and rustle their silvery leaves as if in jealousy of the sheltered, dusty pine down the drive.

Bannockburn is a place visited all year round. In winter the verandah is filled with boxes of driftwood and pinecones for the fire. Frost coats everything in the early morning and the birds are too cold to sing their songs. The old bathtub is frozen and the tadpoles are long gone, pursuing froggy futures in the swamp. Wet clothes left out on the lines are turned to cardboard.

67

ISBN 9780170195935

6   Draw the house at Bannockburn amid the surrounding environment using the details from the passage. We've given you the base to make it easier for you. Remember there are many clues to the setting that are not found in the comparisons. Read the passage carefully to help you. Also try to think of the colours and so on you would use to give your image mood.

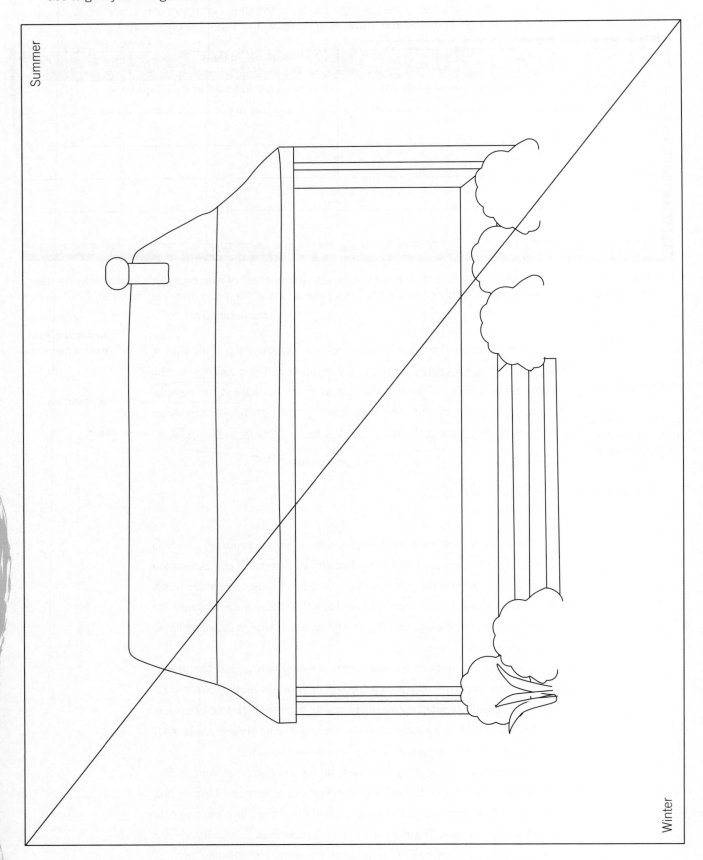

Summer

Winter

7   Now the obvious thing would be to give it a go yourself. Think of a favourite place you have and craft a similar piece of writing. Write the final copy of your piece in the back of this book.

ISBN 9780170195935

Use the following pages to help keep your work in one place. We suggest you use refill for any planning and drafting, and use this space for your final product. Don't forget to date and reference the appropriate unit and page number.

ISBN 9780170195935

Use the following pages to help keep your work in one place. We suggest you use refill for any planning and drafting, and use this space for your final product. Don't forget to date and reference the appropriate unit and page number.

ISBN 9780170195935

ISBN 9780170195935

Use the following pages to help keep your work in one place. We suggest you use refill for any planning and drafting, and use this space for your final product. Don't forget to date and reference the appropriate unit and page number.

ISBN 9780170195935

ISBN 9780170195935

Use the following pages to help keep your work in one place. We suggest you use refill for any planning and drafting, and use this space for your final product. Don't forget to date and reference the appropriate unit and page number.

ISBN 9780170195935

Use the following pages to help keep your work in one place. We suggest you use refill for any planning and drafting, and use this space for your final product. Don't forget to date and reference the appropriate unit and page number.

ISBN 9780170195935

ISBN 9780170195935

Use the following pages to help keep your work in one place. We suggest you use refill for any planning and drafting, and use this space for your final product. Don't forget to date and reference the appropriate unit and page number.

ISBN 9780170195935

ISBN 9780170195935

ISBN 9780170195935